THE GENERAL COUNCILS OF THE CHURCH

THE
General Councils
OF
THE CHURCH

JOHN L. MURPHY

THE BRUCE PUBLISHING COMPANY
MILWAUKEE

NIHIL OBSTAT:

John A. Schulien, S.T.D.
Censor librorum

IMPRIMATUR:

✠ William E. Cousins
Archbishop of Milwaukee

November 19, 1959

Library of Congress Catalog Card Number: 60–8237

TO

MONSIGNOR PETER LEO JOHNSON, D.D.

Foreword

To CERTAIN generations is given the singular privilege of witnessing a great event in ecclesiastical history. Our present generation is one of those so favored. Only twenty times in the long history of the Church have men witnessed a General or Ecumenical Council. Entire centuries have passed without viewing this special facet of the Church's life.

Now, in response to the desire of Pope John XXIII, preparations have begun for the twenty-first such Council. This will most certainly be one of the great events in history. The interest surrounding the Council, however, has also turned our minds back to the past, to the twenty preceding General Councils. Where were they held? At what time? For what reason? What effect did they have?

The purpose of THE GENERAL COUNCILS OF THE CHURCH is to answer some of these questions. What we have tried to do is take a quick glance at the various Councils, and outline, in some way, their place in the history of the Church. A study of the Ecumenical Councils is, in fact, a study of the Church. They have always been closely associated with the great problems that faced the Church and the momentous decisions that had to be made.

There is a certain difficulty involved in summing up nearly 2000 years of history. The reader may feel overwhelmed by a mass of names and dates; but this is unavoidable. It is perhaps best to read the present volume chapter by chapter, noting the chief concerns of each period. At the end, a more unified view may result.

As it is, the characters change from one chapter to another,

Foreword

and at times even within a single chapter. Popes and emperors appear with the same names and different numbers, all of which adds to the confusion. Ultimately, however, it is not the names and dates that matter. Of greater importance are the particular problems that faced the Church in each century. It is these that give a special meaning to the General Councils.

The single unifying element in all these chapters is the Spirit of Christ, who dwells always within His Mystical Body. Externally, the Councils tell a fascinating story. At times, they present a picture of great confusion as well as great harmony. In every instance, however, the Spirit of Christ has triumphed, and the Church has gained much from these twenty solemn gatherings, marked in a special manner by the finger of God.

❋   ❋   ❋   ❋

I would like to take this opportunity to thank those who have assisted me in preparing this volume, above all, the Reverend Robert J. Novotny, S.T.L., and the Reverend Thomas F. Casey, H.E.D., who were most helpful in preparing the manuscript. Their worthwhile suggestions have solved many a problem and clarified a good number of obscure passages.

Contents

[ix]

THE GENERAL COUNCILS OF THE CHURCH

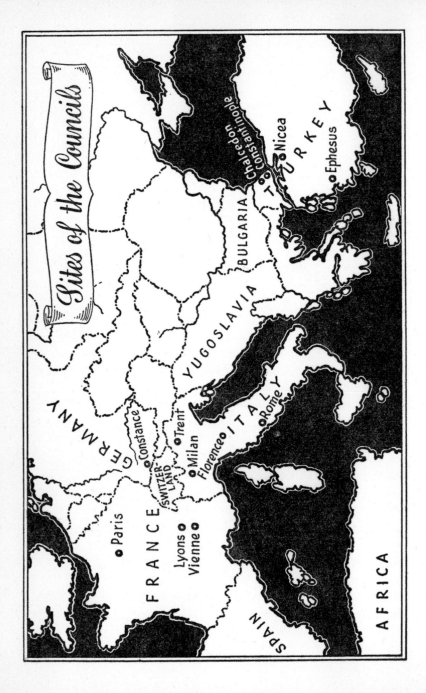

Sites of the Councils

CHAPTER I . . . *Christian Landmarks*

THERE are two ways a man might view the Church of Christ. He might look at it from the "outside," and see it only as an organization. He may think of it as a political body of some sort, or a social group, or even identify it with the priests and bishops and consider it the means of dominating other people. But in every instance his interest in the Church is limited to the human element alone. He sees nothing but a group of "men," not unlike any other organization around him.

The man of faith, on the other hand, will look at the Church from "within." He will see it as the Church of God, the Body of Christ. It is for him a God-directed organization, sustained by the activity of its divine Soul, the Holy Spirit Himself.

This second view gives the only adequate explanation of what the Church is. Beneath the outer appearances of humanity, beneath even the sinfulness and failure of its members, there is the sustaining power of God. God's strength, not man's, has preserved this Church for nearly two thousand years, linking it to the apostolic faith of the primitive community.

The history of the Catholic Church, then, is really a spiritual history: the account of how the Holy Spirit has sustained it

[1]

through the centuries; of how, in His own manner, He has enabled it to withstand persecutions from without and the errors which threatened it from within. The problems the Church has faced in the past two thousand years would have ruined any purely human organization, yet the Church remains. There has been growth, development — nonessential change. But the faith, the sacraments have remained untouched. The power of the Holy Spirit has triumphed over the trials of time.

Central in this long history of the Church's life stand the twenty General (or Ecumenical) Councils. A study of the Councils is, in fact, a study of the Church's history — of the doctrinal and disciplinary problems that have beset her. The Councils stand out as high points in her history, as true Christian landmarks, serving as guides for the future. In every instance, they endeavored to sum up the teaching of the past and to blot out doctrinal errors. By doing this they also pointed out the path to be trod in the days that lay ahead.

The influence of these General Councils has possibly been felt more with the passing of time than it was at the moment of solemn closing. When the color and ceremonial and even the open disputes had vanished, and the bishops and prelates had returned to their own countries, then it was that the Councils really began to exert their influence. Despite all problems, the true doctrine had been set forth, the reforms had been outlined and were now to be incorporated into the lives of the faithful. The influence of such a Council, then, is never felt fully in a day or a month or even years; but it is recognized as a special force in the life of the Church.

The secret behind this special force of a General Council is the Holy Spirit. There have been many local meetings or councils during the long history of the Church. Only twenty similar gatherings, however, stand apart from the others as General or Ecumenical Councils. The underlying reason is the relationship of a General Council to the Holy Spirit. It is, over and above any other ecclesiastical meeting, a particularly profound and solemn expression of the guidance of that Spirit of Truth which Christ promised to send upon His Church:

"If you love me, keep my commandments. And I will ask the Father and he will give you another Advocate to dwell with you forever, the Spirit of Truth whom the world cannot receive, because it neither sees him nor knows him. But you shall know him, because he will dwell with you, and be in you" (Jn. 14:15).

This is the mystery of the Church, the mystery of the General Council. The man of faith can view the Church "from within," because he can perceive the working of the Holy Spirit in the men and women who form the Church. But to the outsider, to the man who does not recognize this divine Soul — who "neither sees Him nor knows Him" — there remains only the outer shell.

Looked at from within, the General Council is not just another meeting. It is different from all other gatherings within the Church. It is the most solemn expression of the doctrinal and disciplinary life of the infallible Church of Christ on earth, "the pillar and mainstay of truth."

As a result, we may say that in these Ecumenical Councils God has visited His people in a special manner. In them the Holy Spirit has shown forth His power in an extraordinary fashion. Christ, the divine Head of the Church, has willed to gather together His bishops, in union with His vicar on earth and under the direction of the Holy Spirit, in order to guide the universal Church. In every General Council, the Mystical Body of Christ repeats this intimate collaboration with the Spirit of Truth which animates it. At the close, the bishops can repeat with the Apostles at Jerusalem: "For the Holy Spirit and we have decided. . . ."

The difference between a General Council, then, and a local council, is not to be sought primarily in the legal requirements upon which they are based. The current laws of the Church only formulate, in their own way, the deeper theological truth. The true meaning of a General Council arises from the intimate nature of the Church established by Christ.

In other words, it is not fundamentally a question of how many bishops must attend, or from what parts of the world they must actually come, or by what papal decree they are approved. These are important questions, of course. But it is the supernatural life of the Church which gives meaning to them all. A General Council is a part of the "mystery" of the Church. Like all the varied elements within the Church, it also shares in the supernatural quality of that life. It is far more than a gathering together of bishops in a certain place; it is far more than solemnity and color. It is, above all this, a *special manifestation of the Holy Spirit,* ever dwelling within this Church of Christ.

As a glance at the list of General Councils will indicate, they have been celebrated in many different places, under many and diverse circumstances. There has been great variety in the external ceremony and color. The number of bishops who attended has varied greatly, ranging from as few as one hundred to as many as one thousand bishops and prelates. Some Councils have continued for years; others have been completed in a matter of days. Some were great spectacles before the world, causing comment on all sides; others were celebrated in such fashion that large parts of the Catholic world scarcely knew that they were going on. The single thread that joins them together, however, is this special working of the Holy Spirit which comes into play at an Ecumenical Council.

There must, of course, be certain laws concerning such a Council. It is not up to every individual to decide whether a particular Council is or is not an Ecumenical Council. When the Holy Father, for example, gives to the Church a solemn definition (like the definition of the Assumption in 1950), we

[4]

can also see beneath this the special working of the Holy Spirit. The Pope, however, must still make clear to the Church that he *intends* to speak infallibly; he must let the members know that this is to be a solemn definition.

So also with a General Council: there must be some way of knowing that it *is* a General Council. The Church must make clear to its members that this is to be an Ecumenical, and not a local, Council, so that they may perceive in it this special manifestation of the Holy Spirit.

Thus we have the legal requirements established for setting up a General Council. To be truthful, some of these technical requirements seem to have varied through the centuries. The Church can establish the laws which seem most fitting for the circumstances in which she finds herself. The history of some of these twenty Councils is shrouded in a good amount of obscurity. Special questions may be raised concerning precisely who first called the Council together, who attended it, and what its precise relationship to the Bishop of Rome might have been. But in the life of the Church, the matter shines forth with much more clarity. The Church of Christ is a living thing, and as such it grasps in a living fashion the activity of the Holy Spirit within it.

Thus the Church has *de facto* recognized certain Councils as ecumenical. The decrees of these gatherings have played a special role in the life of Christ's members. If we look over the general history of them all, we are able to draw certain conclusions about what makes a General Council. It is from a consideration of all these various elements that we come to our present-day understanding of such a Council.

If we were to define it, our definition would run something like this: "A General Council is a legitimate gathering of the bishops of the entire world, called for the purpose of discussing and settling the doctrinal and disciplinary questions of the universal Church." A closer look at this definition will explain more fully the nature of a General Council.

It is first of all a "legitimate" gathering. As Christ established His Church, there are to be always and everywhere bishops who rule their dioceses in the same way in which the Pope rules the universal Church. These bishops are not simply the Pope's "representatives" in the diocese. They rule in the place of Christ, by divine right. They are, therefore, Christ's "local vicars," as it were. While their power to rule comes *from God,* however, it is also true that they receive it *through* the Pope. And this is important.

The bishops of the world and the Roman Pontiff form together the "college of bishops." Cardinal Billot compared them to a human person: the head and members being the Pope and the other bishops. They act in a Council as one unit, setting forth one teaching, one solemn judgment.

A universal gathering of bishops, however, can never be "legitimate" without the head — the Roman Pontiff. This springs from the very nature of the Church as Christ established it. The Pope, therefore, must in some way preside over every General Council; this is his office by the will of God and it cannot be set aside.

There still can be a question of exactly what this involves for the Pope. In giving their answers, writers will phrase them in different ways, using various distinctions. But the over-all response is much the same.

It does not seem that the Roman Pontiff must "call together" the General Council in the sense that he *starts* the entire procedure. (Some writers will speak of this as the "material convocation" — that is, the actual sending out of invitations, and the like.) Today, of course, this is always true, but history seems to indicate that such was not the case in the early centuries, where the emperor seems to have taken the first official step.

The teaching both of the Church and of history tells us, however, that no General Council has been called against the wishes of the Supreme Pontiff, and without his solemn approval. It is this approval of the "head" that gives to the entire proceedings the nature of a legitimate Council. Without it, there would not be the authority required, nor this special manifestation of the Holy Spirit we talked about. This the authors will call the "formal convocation," that is, the official, authoritative "calling together" of this group precisely as a General Council. Unless this takes place at some time, there is no such Council, even though the actual *meetings* might take place.

In practice, this approval (or "formal convocation") has generally been given *before* the Council actually meets; but it may occur *simultaneously* with the meetings themselves, or it can even *follow* the actual gathering. Moreover, the Roman Pontiff may show his approval in any number of ways: by solemnly calling the Council, or by addressing an official letter to the group; or by sending his delegates to attend; or by signifying his approval at the completion of the discussions.

In any event, no final decree of a Council is binding unless the Roman Pontiff approves of that final form. This, again, springs from the very nature of the Church. A Council is a gathering of the head and members; but if the head refuses to approve of what the members have done, those particular statements are not decrees of an Ecumenical Council. We shall have occasion to note instances of this as we look at the Councils of the past.

A General Council will also include the "bishops of the entire world." This, again, must not be understood to indicate that the actual "celebration" of the Council demands that every bishop really be present. Morally speaking, bishops should be present from all parts of the world, but the emphasis is to be placed on another fact. In a General Council, all the bishops have a *right* to take a seat in the deliberations; they belong there. This will appear above all in the official approval of the Council by the Roman Pontiff which will signify the intention or purpose of the Council to legislate for the *universal* Church. This would not be true, let us say, of a particular or local council, where only the bishops attached to the dioceses concerned would have the right to be present. In other words, it is not simply a question of counting bishops until they are all present, or until a majority of some sort has arrived. Such a Council is not any more "universal" if 2000 bishops attend than if only 200 are present. It is not a question of numbers.

Externally, of course, a General Council ought to express this "universality" by the actual attendance of bishops from all over the world; most frequently this has been the case. But this is *not* the precise point that makes such a Council "ecumenical" or "universal." (Ecumenical comes from the Greek word *oikoumenē*, meaning "the inhabited world"; thus the entire world: "universal.")

This notion is also expressed in the definition by the words: "called for the purpose of discussing and settling the doctrinal and disciplinary questions of the universal Church." The concern of a General Council is not simply a particular locality; it is the faith and practice of the entire Church throughout the whole world. For this reason, its decrees will have a greater meaning than any local Council. Ultimately, however, it is the manifestation of the Holy Spirit in a special fashion that makes this so. Only in a General Council is the Spirit of Truth active in this extraordinary manner. For this reason *only* a General Council can decree for the universal Church; and the decrees only of a General Council are infallible. A local or particular council of bishops is not infallible; it does not carry with it the promise of freedom from error. A General Council, on the other hand, called together as a moral person — head and members (the Roman Pontiff and the bishops of the world) — enjoys the same infallibility as a solemn definition of the Roman Pontiff himself.

It is, thus, the infallible Church which is the primary concern. In setting forth the revealed truth, this Church cannot fall into error. Since the Church possesses official teachers, however, this infallible statement can come about in various ways: (1) It may be evidenced in the day-to-day teaching of the bishops throughout the world, teaching the same doctrine, in union with the Supreme Pontiff. (2) It may also be evidenced in a solemn statement of the successor of Peter himself — in what we now call an *ex cathedra* statement, that is, issued "from the throne." (3) However, the Church may also speak infallibly in a legitimate General Council. In every instance, the Church has the assurance that these statements will not be erroneous. They will be true guides for the Christian, bringing him a clearer understanding of the message of Christ, and helping him to serve his Master more faithfully and more perfectly.

In all of this, we see the action of the Holy Spirit, ever dwelling within the Church. If we turn now to a closer look at the individual Councils of the Universal Church, we will be able to see how, under the guidance of this Spirit of Truth, the Church has been able to meet the problems of the ages.

The first conciliar landmark dates from the fourth century: the Council of Nicea (325). It was especially concerned with the Trinity, and for the next three hundred years or so, other General Councils would arise, dealing with this same question. In this fashion, the Church arrived at a more precise statement of the truths concerning Christ and the Trinity.

In the Middle Ages, new problems would demand attention. There was the question of reform within the Church, and that of reunion with those who had drifted away from it. At one point in history, the Councils had to deal especially with the papacy itself when the entire Church was thrown into confusion by the claims of pseudo-popes. The Protestant Revolt of the sixteenth century would bring forth the great Council of Trent; and the problems of our modern world had to be answered in the Vatican Council of the past century.

All of these, one by one, took their place in the list of great Councils, through which Christ spoke again and again to His people. Even if they seemed, at times, to fail in the achievement of their immediate goal, the directives were there — the voice of Christ was heard. Because of the special influence of the Holy Spirit in these most solemn gatherings, they were destined to overshadow the many local councils and synods held during these same centuries. And this is the mystery of the Councils, the role of these Christian landmarks. By the will of God, they were destined, each in its own way, to shine forth as beacons, directing the life of the Church and outlining through the darkness the path to be followed by the faithful members of Christ upon earth.

CHAPTER II . . . *The Church Before Nicea*

WHEN Christ walked the earth with His disciples, preaching to the people, He unfolded clearly for the first time the sublime mystery of the Trinity. The mind of man stood helpless before this revelation. It could never grasp this truth completely. In fact, until God Himself opened up to the mind of man the secret of the Trinitarian life, no one could have even imagined the divine nature being shared equally by three divine Persons. Yet this was, above all, the mystery revealed by Christ. It was the mystery of Christ Himself: God the Son among men, come to save them from their sin.

It was to be the work of the Church on earth to continue the work of Christ. Aided by His Spirit, it was to keep alive and unchanged the truth unveiled by God; acting as His instrument, it was to share in the work of applying to the souls of men the graces won for them upon Calvary. For this reason, the history of the Church is really the history of Christ — Christ in His fullness, the Mystical Christ.

The early years of that history were troubled years. They were dominated by two chief concerns. There were on the one hand, the recurring persecutions from without, and, on the other, the doctrinal errors within. The doctrinal battles had to be carried on while the men and women who believed in Christ passed through the terrors of persecution. This was the special cross of the first few centuries.

Sometimes our modern view of the ancient Church may tend to exaggerate the nature of the persecutions. Unless we are careful, we may come to think of the Christians of the first few centuries as living constantly in the catacombs, and coming into the light of day only to meet the beasts in the martyr's arena. Actually, the persecutions were not a continual, relentless persecution of the followers of Christ. They were more periodic, interspaced with years of relative peace. But they did keep returning, again and again, until the end of the third century. In the background of these persecutions, especially in the years of peace, the Church continued to grow, became more definitely organized, and set forth its doctrine with ever increasing clarity.

The first persecution broke out soon after the death of Christ, in Jerusalem itself. It was this that first helped the faith to spread to other parts of the known world, for the Christians had to leave Jerusalem. This persecution under Agrippa, which must have begun about the year 36, brought the Church its first martyr, St. Stephen.

This, however, was only a faint echo of the two particularly fierce persecutions which marked that first century. The Roman emperors also turned their hatred against the Christians. First there was the persecution of Nero (from A.D. 64 to 67), and then — after twenty-five years of relative peace — that of Domitian (A.D. 95).

Yet these two trials were only the beginning. In the next century, Rome continued to persecute the followers of Christ. There was, however, one difference. In the second century, the emperors paid more attention to the legal requirements for condemning Christians. This was, of course, scant comfort to those who died "legally." It was, nevertheless, the first step toward a change in official attitude. Thus, while these later emperors were not exactly "friends" of the Church, their attitude was different enough that Tertullian could write that only Nero and Domitian were the "enemies" of the Christians.

Nevertheless, the persecutions did continue; Clement of Rome and Ignatius of Antioch died under Trajan at the beginning of the second century. Hadrian, Antoninus, and Marcus Aurelius all continued to bring Christians to trial and to punish them with death. Polycarp, the bishop of Smyrna, died under Antoninus, in 156; the church at Lyons was all but blotted out under Marcus Aurelius, only to rise again under the direction of Irenaeus.

The first real help came from the worst of the Roman emperors (from the *Roman* point of view). Commodus (180–192) was very little interested in enforcing the Roman law, but from this the Christians benefited. It was still against the law to be a Christian, but the State under Commodus was not too much concerned with that fact.

With the death of Commodus, matters took on a different color once again. Under Septimius Severus (193–211), the State began to take the initiative in bringing Christians to trial. Formerly, the State had waited for denunciations from the people. In practice, however, this change resulted in even more sporadic persecutions. They arose more suddenly, at the will of the Emperor; they were in some ways more violent. Eventually they died out, one by one, having spent their force with no lasting effect. Septimius Severus failed in his attempt to slow down the progress of Christianity. Nor did the bloody persecution of Maximin (235–238), brief though it was, meet with any greater success. The Christian Church remained.

In the middle of the 3rd century, with the coming of Decius (249), we came upon the last — and the most violent — persecution of the century. This general persecution aimed at stamping out the Christians once and for all. During this period large numbers of Christians apostatized. The persecution was waged on all sides: at Rome, in Africa, in Gaul, in Spain, and in Asia; Christians died by the hundreds. Gallus succeeded Decius in 251 and renewed the persecution.

Valerian, the successor of Gallus, continued this policy soon after he became emperor (253–260). It was only after his death that it appeared the trials were over. But the appearances were deceptive. After nearly twenty years of peace, Diocletian was instigated by Galerius to undertake what was to be the final persecution of the Christians (303). A period of violence followed, with many deaths, but Christianity was to triumph. The bloody purge was finally called off in 311 by Constantine, Licinius and Galerius — one of the very men who had moved Diocletian to begin it. It was now stated officially (even though begrudgingly) that "it is permissible to be a Christian." Church property was restored, religious assemblies were allowed.

The final and lasting peace came with the famous Edict of Milan in 313: the peace of Constantine. It marks the dividing point in the history of the early Church, and brings with it the first General Council of Nicea.

With these external trials as a backdrop, the doctrinal battle went on within the Church during these same years. Before St. Paul died, he wrote a letter to his disciple Timothy, summing up the Christian teaching: "Remember that Jesus Christ rose from the dead and was descended from David; this is my gospel, in which I suffer even to bonds, as a criminal" (2 Tim. 2:8). These two points were the extremes which had been joined together in Christ. He is a true Man: descended from David; but He is also God, since He rose from the dead as He had foretold. The whole doctrinal story of the early Church is a defense of these two extremes against those who would overemphasize one point at the expense of the other.

Even before the first century had drawn to a close, there were those who had begun to challenge this central thought of Christianity. For different reasons, they denied especially that Christ was true God. When St. John wrote the Fourth Gospel toward the end of the first century, he clearly had them in mind. He explains this as the very reason why he wrote his Gospel: "But these are written that you may believe that Jesus is the Christ, the Son of God . . ." (Jn. 20:31).

There were also some men who denied that Christ was the Messias; these were, especially, the early Christians who belonged to the so-called "Judaizing" party. They wished to hold fast to the practices of the old Jewish Law, and yet they realized that there was in the teaching of Christ a certain rejection of at least part of this Law. In rejecting Him as the Messias, however, they also rejected Him as God.

Other Christians of the first century came into contact with systems of philosophy that taught that material things were evil in themselves. They believed in Christ, but came to deny that He was true Man. Because of these other ideas, they felt they had to deny at once that Christ ever possessed a real, physical body. To them it seemed impossible that "God" could have taken on something as "evil" as a material, physical body.

St. Ignatius of Antioch, put to death at the beginning of the second century, was greatly concerned with those who denied that Christ possessed a true human nature. On his journey to Rome, where he was to die, he wrote seven letters to different churches. In them he mentions the error of these men. We now refer to them as "Docetists," from the Greek word *dokein* (which means "to seem" or "to appear"). They claimed that Christ only "seemed" to have a body like ours; actually He did not. Hence Ignatius wrote: "Be deaf, then, to any talk that ignores Jesus Christ, of David's lineage, of Mary: who was really born, ate, and drank; was really persecuted under Pontius Pilate; was really crucified and died, in the sight of heaven and earth and the underworld. He was really raised from the dead, for his Father raised him, just as his Father will raise us. . . . It is not as some unbelievers say, that his Passion was a sham. It is they who are a sham! Yes, and their fate will fit their fancies — they will be ghosts and apparitions."

The men of this period eventually began to speak of the Trinity by using terms that differ from those in Scripture. This, of course, was something that had to happen. The doctrinal history of the Church is a continuation of this process. What has been said in the graphic speech of Scripture must come to be expressed in more "technical" terms to satisfy the needs of the inquiring mind of man, and to answer the objections of various heretics. This could not be avoided. But when man attempts to explain in any way the content of revealed truth, there is the grave danger that he will distort it. He may all too easily put his ideas into the words of Scripture, and give them an entirely new meaning.

Ultimately, only the proper teaching authority in the Church can give the final answer. This is the task of the Popes and the General Councils down through the ages: to single out what is a valid clarification of scriptural terminology from what is erroneous. Without the guarantee of an infallible guide in this matter, Christian truth would soon be lost in the maze of contrary opinions. Yet, we need not believe the opinion of any mere man, no matter how wise nor how saintly he may be. We are obliged to accept on faith only the word of God, and nothing more. For this reason God continues to speak through His Church. He makes use of those to whom He has entrusted the sacred office of teaching. They speak not on their authority, but on God's and we accept not their opinion but the truth testified by the authority of God who speaks through them.

Before such matters are settled, however, history recounts a long series of errors and confusions. An infallible teaching authority does not receive a new revelation from heaven. Though guided always by the Holy Spirit, the Popes and the bishops of the world have not always known what to say. They must discuss and study the truths of faith, and only then can they speak. Infallibility at that moment means that when they do speak, God will keep them from error.

Thus in these early years, we see the need of stating the very same truth of Scripture, but by expressing it in different words. In that way, the Church comes to understand revealed truth more clearly. Later, for example, we will note how the Blessed Mother is solemnly defined, at the Council of Ephesus, as the "Mother of God." This is said nowhere in Scripture in these very words; but it is true nevertheless. It is contained *in* Scripture, just as the belief in it was a part of the faith and teaching of the Church in the first century. But it must gradually be stated in these more precise terms.

Perhaps the first great impulse toward this process came from the Gnostics. *Gnosis* means "knowledge," and these were the "wise ones" who claimed to understand life properly. There were pagan Gnostics before Christ; thus Gnosticism did not develop from Christianity. When some of these men came into contact with Christian truth, however, they attempted to join the two teachings together. Frequently they fell into error. Their fundamental belief that matter is evil was at the basis of the error of "Docetism," into which some of them fell — the belief that Christ had no true physical body.

The Gnostics also thought of God as someone from whom there came forth "sparks" of some sort — emanations, they called them. This notion was to confuse the Christians of later centuries when they came to describe the relationship of the Second Person of the Trinity to the Father. In fact, the general Gnostic notions will occasionally appear in our doctrinal history for many centuries. Gnosticism developed many varied forms, so that it is really impossible to reduce them all to one system. But the general tendencies are clear when they do appear.

As a result, the early defenders of the faith were especially concerned with these and similar errors. In regard to the explanation of Christian faith in the third century two men stand out: Tertullian and Origen. These two had a tremendous effect on the "technical" vocabulary which the Church was developing — Tertullian in Latin, Origen in Greek. New words had to be coined to express the truths of the Christian faith in something beyond the words of Scripture, and they helped lead the way.

By departing from the graphic terms of Scripture, however, they were taking a certain risk, and eventually they both fell into a doctrinal error. Tertullian even left the Church and joined the group known as Montanists — a group of Christians who desired to lead extremely devout lives, but who fell into error since they felt they alone were being guided by the Holy Spirit; the Church itself had supposedly fallen into serious heresy.

In the third century, however, new errors began to rise, errors that can be identified in special ways. They were actually preparing the way for *the* heresy of the early Church: *Arianism*. The names of two men stand out in this early period: Sabellius and Paul of Samosata.

Sabellius was a priest of Lybia who taught chiefly at Rome. He attempted to explain the Trinity in a novel fashion: he admitted only a *difference in names*. Thus, he claimed, whenever we speak of the Father, the Son, and the Holy Spirit, we are really only calling the one divine Person by three different names, depending on how God is manifesting Himself to the Church. Sabellius has the dubious honor (given to others throughout the centuries) of having this general error named after him: *Sabellianism*. There were, however, other men who held similar teachings, and other names. One group was known as the *Patripassiani*. They logically concluded that if there was only a difference in names, it was really the "Father" who suffered on the cross. Hence the name, from *Pater* (father) and *passio* (suffer).

Paul of Samosata was the bishop of Antioch, and an important name in history, since he was a friend of Lucian, the teacher of Arius. Paul of Samosata taught things very much like Sabellius, but he attempted to explain the teaching in more scientific fashion. His starting place was God as an intelligent Being. God has intelligence, and therefore He can "utter" a divine *word*. This word he called by the Greek name *Logos*, which means the same thing. For Paul, however, this *Logos* was not a person at all; it was only a manner in which God manifested His power.

As a result, when Paul of Samosata came to speak of Christ, he claimed that Christ was only a man — a mere man, and nothing more. He was not God. We might call him the "adopted son" of God, but for Paul that meant only one thing: this "power" of God (the *Logos*) overshadowed Jesus, and dwelt in Him as in a temple.

In this teaching, the *Logos* is not really "distinct" from God; it is simply an impersonal power of God. Thus the *Logos* was not a divine person. Paul of Samosata expressed this by saying that God and the *Logos* were "of one substance." In saying this, he used a most important word in the history of the Church, but used it in his own meaning: *homo-ousion*. As Paul of Samosata used it, it meant there was no Trinity of persons at all — no Father and Son (nor Holy Spirit). The *Logos* was simply an attribute or power of God. In this he was very much like Sabellius.

To this, however, Paul had added another idea: the notion

of the *Logos* coming to dwell in Jesus of Nazareth. In this way he was helping to prepare for the big debate of the Council of Nicea, for Arius was to develop this thought in his own way.

With the stage set in this fashion, two new figures appear who are destined to bring forth the first General Council of the Church. The one is Constantine, the Emperor who would give peace and official recognition to the Church. The other is Arius, who by his teaching on the Trinity, would succeed in tearing asunder the Church of Christ, and bring forth the need of a General Council. He was to do it, however, not by persecution from without, but by sowing the seeds of doctrinal error within the Church itself.

CHAPTER III . . . *Council of Nicea*

IN THE Church of the fourth century, there were two centers
of intellectual life that have assumed a special place in history:
Antioch and Alexandria. Both of these cities had their own
schools in which Christianity was discussed and analyzed, and
both cities developed their own approach. When we speak of
them today, we think more of the "spirit" behind each school,
rather than the school itself. It was the special approach of
each that determined their influence.

Antioch was one of the largest cities of the Roman Empire,
surpassed only by Rome and Alexandria. It was one of the
most beautiful cities of the East, a center of Greek culture; yet
it marked the border line between the two worlds, the East
and the West. Oriental mysticism mingled there with the more
legal spirit of Rome. It was here that Peter had first settled,
before moving on to Rome; on February 22 the Church cele-
brates this in the feast of the "Chair of St. Peter at Antioch."
And as St. Luke informs us, ". . . it was in Antioch that the
disciples were first called 'Christians'" (Acts 11:26).

In the fourth century, there was a learned man at Antioch
who exercised so great an influence over Christian thought that

he is usually called the founder of the "School of Antioch." This man was Lucian. The name of Diodorus of Tarsus also marks a high point of the school, as well as St. John Chrysostom, the great preacher-bishop of Constantinople, who also had received his training at Antioch.

The spirit of Antioch laid special emphasis upon the grammatical and historical meaning of Scripture, and on the value of human reason in the service of religion. This carried with it, unfortunately, the special danger of falling into a purely historical and rational approach to Christian truth. History and human reason tended to mark the approach of Antioch more than they ought to. The end result was a number of heresies in which Scripture was understood more by human reason than according to the traditional faith of the Church.

Alexandria, on the other hand, was the great port city of Egypt. Even before the time of Christ, it included a large Jewish population, a group that showed a special concern for combining Jewish culture with Greek philosophy. To meet the needs especially of the Egyptian Jews, the Greek translation of the Old Testament was made — the Septuagint, as it is called.

The Christians of Alexandria in the fourth century shared much of this same spirit. As in Antioch, there were certain catechetical schools established in the third century. The greatest name associated with these schools in northern Africa is that of Origen. His influence was such that he is justly looked upon as the great light of the Alexandrian school; he was active in this city about the year 215 under Clement of Alexandria.

Somewhat in opposition to Antioch, the school of Alexandria adopted a more philosophical or even mystical approach to Christian truth. In explaining Scripture, this latter school tended to see imagery or allegory in the inspired texts, and showed less concern than did Antioch for the literal sense of Scripture. This approach carried with it another special danger, the danger of falling into some kind of exaggerated "spiritualism." It could produce a manner of speaking of the Church that tended to wander off from the visible reality of daily life. Despite this, the followers of Origen time and again rose to defend the orthodox teaching of the Church. Of them all, St. Athanasius stands out as the greatest. The history of this most famous bishop of Alexandria is intimately linked up with the story of Arius and Arianism.

In the fourth century, and in the centuries to follow, the theological disputes were to center in a special way in these two schools, Antioch and Alexandria. The pendulum swings first to one side, then to the other. Out of the conflict came the clear statements of the early Councils of the Church.

When Lucian began his teaching at Antioch, he sowed the seeds of the greatest error concerning Christ in the early Church, Arianism. Lucian had been a friend and ally of Paul of Samosata, and he carried with him many similar ideas. Paul had really held that there was no Trinity. The *Logos* (the "power" of God, as he understood it) had simply "dwelt" in the man, Jesus of Nazareth. Lucian held something similar, and passed it on to his most famous pupil at the school of Antioch — a priest by the name of Arius.

Arius was a native of Libya but was attached to the church of Alexandria. He evidently studied at Antioch under Lucian; at any rate, his doctrine is assuredly inspired by that of Lucian. Arianism breathes the spirit of Antioch even though it came to light in Alexandria; it was, moreover, accepted very quickly by the school of Antioch while failing to capture Alexandria or Egypt throughout the fourth century. In its concern for the literal meaning of Scripture, and its deceptive use of the arguments of human reason, Arianism reflects the approach of Antioch rather than the allegory of Alexandria.

As a heresy, Arianism was not "popular" in the sense that

the ordinary Christian fully understood the complicated system. It was above all a concern of the schools. It is a curious fact of history, however, that this heresy did filter down into the market place, and became the topic of daily conversation and the subject matter of popular songs and hymns. What this really amounted to was more of a "taking sides" on the part of the people — particularly when the political decrees of the emperors added to the conflict. To be a "good Arian," as far as the man in the street was concerned, often meant to be a devoted follower of some strong leader. This very fact contributed much to the progress of Arianism, just as it did later on with regard to Protestantism in the sixteenth century.

Arius himself was an excellent example of such a strong leader. He was well known as a preacher, and had a large following among a certain class of Christians at Alexandria. He was able to gather about him men and women who were especially interested in leading a more perfect or penitential form of life. Into his preaching, however, he gradually introduced more and more of Lucian's theory about the Son of God. This could not fail to attract the attention of the bishop of Alexandria, a man named Alexander. About 318 the bishop began an inquiry into the manner in which Arius explained Christ as the Son of God. When he recognized the teaching of Arius for what it was, he saw how much it was opposed to the faith handed down by the Apostles. Arius was therefore called upon to give up this teaching once and for all. When he refused to do so, he was excommunicated by the bishop, along with his followers, most likely in 319 or 320.

The theory of Arius is difficult to express briefly. His interpretation of one scriptural text may serve as a starting point. St. Paul had written to the Colossians: "He (Christ) is the image of the invisible God, the *first-born* of every creature. For in him were created all things in the heavens and on the earth . . ." (Col. 1:15). Ignoring all other texts of the Bible, the Arians tried to defend their theory on this and similar phrases.

For Arius, there was but one God and one divine Person. This God is eternal. There is mention in Scripture, however, of not only Christ but also the *Logos:* the "Word." As far as Arius was concerned, this Word (the *Logos*) was not God; he was not the second Person of the Trinity. He was simply a creature, but a creature of a special and unique type. The *Logos*, he claimed, was created by God before everything else; he was created before the world, before the universe, before time. But the *Logos* was created by God, and created out of nothing; thus he is the "first-born of every creature." As a result, however, the *Logos* was not God, and therefore he did not possess the very same nature or being as God. He was not, in other words, of the same "substance" as God.

In Greek the word especially used for substance was *ousia.* The adjective "same" was, in Greek, *homos.* It is from this Greek word that we have such English words as "homogenized." Homogenized milk, for example, is milk that is all of "one and the same kind" (from *homos* and *genos* – "kind"). Thus *homo-ousia* means "one and the same substance."

The Arians would not admit this truth; what they were really denying, of course, was the divinity of Christ. If the *Logos* was not of the same nature, the same substance as God, then he was not God. And this is just what they taught.

There was a time, then, when the *Logos* did not exist. He was created by the free will of God. According to Arius, however, this *Logos* became in turn the creator of all other things in the universe. Thus the Word was more of a superangel, as it were, the first and highest creature of God; in fact, the *Logos* was the only creature directly created by God. In this sense only is he called by Scripture the "only-begotten." All other things were created directly by the *Logos* and not by God. This does give other creatures some kind of reason for calling the *Logos* "God." He brought them into existence.

This must be understood as "God" only in a secondary sense, however. Arius would admit that the *Logos*, as a creature, could have sinned; this could not be true of God. Since the Father foresaw from all eternity that the Logos would not sin, He "adopted" the *Logos* in a special manner as His Son. Only in this way is the *Logos* God; he is an "adopted God," but nothing more.

Thus when Scripture speaks of the "Son of God," this is all it means, according to Arius. When Paul said that the Word is the "first-born of every creature," and that "in him were created all things," this is how it is to be understood. But there is no real possession of one and the same nature by God and the *Logos*. They differ as the Creator differs from a creature.

The entire matter might have ended when the bishop of Alexandria excommunicated Arius, but it did not. Arius was a proud man, and a man with influential contacts. When he realized that he was in trouble, he sought out protectors, and he found them. Thus the conflict was extended. His most powerful defender was a fellow disciple of Lucian; it was Eusebius, by this time bishop of the imperial city of Nicomedia. He was a man of great power, and eventually Arius fled to Nicodemia, having left Alexandria. There he experienced the protection of Eusebius; from Nicomedia he carried on his defense.

A period of letter writing soon followed. Arius wrote those bishops he hoped would defend him; some of his bishop-patrons wrote other bishops, trying to win them over to the position of Arius. The bishop of Alexandria, however, also wrote to the other bishops — more than 70 letters in all. Among them was a letter to the Pope at Rome, containing an official account of the heretical teaching of Arius, and of his excommunication.

While all of this was going on, Constantine, who had come to power in 306, was gaining ground. In 313, the imperial edict that brought the persecution of the Church to an end bore the names of Galerius, Constantine, and Licinius. Fifteen days after the publication of the decree, Galerius was dead; only Constantine and Licinius remained. In September of 323, however, Constantine defeated the Eastern Emperor, Licinius, and in 324 became at last the sole ruler of the Roman world. And it was to him that the disputing parties now turned for a solution.

Constantine had for some reason chosen as his special ecclesiastical adviser the bishop of the Spanish city of Cordova, a man named Hosius. This bishop may possibly have had something to do with the conversion of Constantine. At any rate, Hosius was destined to play a large role in the first General Council of the Church.

When Constantine had emerged as the sole ruler of the Empire, and had heard of the doctrinal disputes that were going on in the Church, he first of all sent Hosius to the bishop of Alexandria. He had hoped thus to negotiate peace between the disputing parties. Little was accomplished by this mission, but either as a result of it or by reason of later conversations, it was realized that this problem could not be settled at a local level. Hosius had learned the full error of Arius and its terrifying implications for Christian truth. As a solution, the Council of Nicea, the first Christian landmark in the long line of General Councils, came into being.

There had been many smaller "councils" or synods before Nicea; the idea was not entirely new. What was different, however, was the notion of a *General* or *Universal* Council. For the first time the bishops of the entire world were to be gathered together to determine a point of Catholic belief. As the ancient historian Eusebius remarks: "When they were all assembled at

Nicea, it appeared evident that the proceeding was the work of God. . . ." For the first time, the activity of the Holy Spirit in a General Council was to be experienced by the Christian world.

Our knowledge of the Council is rather limited; the accounts of the *Acta* of the gathering are said to have covered some forty volumes, but they have long since been lost. It seems clear, however, that Constantine himself, at the urging of the bishops near him, sent out the invitations to the bishops to attend. Constantine also paid the expenses involved in the celebration of the Council. The primary purpose of the gathering was to solve the problem of Arianism, although two other points were to be discussed: (1) the date for the celebration of Easter, which had been disputed by some; and (2) the question of the schism of Meletius in Egypt — a man who attempted to usurp the power of the bishop of Alexandria in a dispute concerning those who had denied the faith during the persecutions (the *lapsi*).

The Roman Pontiff, Sylvester I, was apparently not consulted before Constantine acted, but he ratified the move by sending two legates to the gathering, the Roman priests Victor and Vincentius. It was in this way that the "head" of the college of bishops convoked the meeting — what the authors refer to as the "formal convocation."

The Council was to be held at Nicea in Bithynia. It was a convenient location for the Western bishops to reach, since it is close to the sea, but the principal reason for the choice seems to have been the desire of the Emperor to attend. Nicea lay close to the summer residence of the Emperor, and it was therefore far more convenient. Today there is nothing at this spot but a small village called Isnik, but at that time, Nicea was the center of the cultural life of Bithynia. Known as the "Golden City," it was a fitting spot for this great spectacle to unfold.

The Council opened, it would seem, about May 20, 325. It apparently closed on June 19. The opening session was a magnificent event, and obviously quite a change for many of the bishops who attended. Some of them had known even personally the final persecutions under Diocletian and, even more recently, under Licinius. They must have flinched as they passed by the armed soldiers, standing now only as honorary guards to add solemnity to the event. Memories of imperial guards in the past, seeking out Christians and leading them to death, could not help but come to mind. But the world had changed very rapidly.

The bishops gathered in the grand hall of the imperial palace at Nicea, where seats had been arranged on opposite sides of the room. Clad as an Oriental sovereign, in gold and precious stones, Constantine entered the hall in solemn fashion once the bishops had gathered together. He then addressed them briefly in Latin on the purpose of the Council, and his talk was immediately translated into Greek. Then the lively debates began among the bishops present.

In all, there were about 250 bishops present. The traditional number given is 318, but this seems to be a reference more to the 318 servants of Abraham than historical record (cf. Gen. 14:14). The Creed itself bears the signature of only 220 bishops. Most of those in attendance came from the eastern half of the Empire, but the Western provinces, Africa, Spain, Gaul, and Italy, were also represented by at least one bishop.

The bishops soon grouped into parties, following their own convictions. There was a small but powerful group of 15 or 20 bishops favoring Arius, led by Eusebius of Nicomedia. A second group urged the solution of stating simply what had been said before, with no further clarification; these included the bishops who disliked the idea of defining faith in new terms not found in Scripture. A third group, however, eventually achieved its desire. These bishops wished to re-examine the entire teaching in the light of tradition, and express Catholic belief clearly, and, if need be, in new terminology.

Arius was given a chance to defend his teaching, but when he expressed his position clearly and bluntly, all but his own party wished to condemn him. It was apparent by then that some kind of formula had to be adopted to do this. Eusebius of Nicomedia, Arius' patron, was ready for this; he had prepared such a formula. As might be expected, it was so vague that both the Catholics and the Arians could sign it with equal ease; it was no solution at all.

Only after overcoming the objections of those who wished to repeat nothing but the scriptural terminology was the final Creed formulated: "We believe in one God, the Father Almighty, Creator of all things visible and invisible. And in one Lord Jesus Christ, the *Son of God,* the only-begotten of the Father, that is, *of the substance of the Father;* God from God, light from light, true God from true God; begotten, *not created, consubstantial* (*homo-ousion*) with the Father. . . ."

The phrase "Son of God" was used in place of *Logos* to avoid any confusion on that point. The words "only-begotten" were further explained as meaning that the Word was not created from nothing, but possessed the very nature and substance of the Father.

It was, however, by describing the Son of God as "of one and the same substance" with the Father — consubstantial — that the Arians were overcome above all. Those who insisted on this word realized this as much as did the Arians themselves. To say that the *Logos* was "of one and the same substance" with the Father meant that he was not simply "from God" or "like God"; it meant that he *is* God in the full sense of the term, identical with the Father. It was thus the ideal means for separating the orthodox believers from the heretics, for to accept this term meant to abandon the teaching of Arius. In this way did *homo-ousion* become the byword of Nicea and the years that lay ahead.

When these formulations were finally settled, all but two of the bishops signed; they were condemned by the Council along with Arius. Even Eusebius of Nicomedia signed. The first General Council came to an end, and before the papal legates and the bishops returned to their homes, the Emperor entertained them at a lavish banquet. Constantine then officially approved the decrees of the Council, and set them forth as laws of the State, ordering the removal of all those who failed to accept these decrees. But the story did not end there; in fact, it was scarcely beginning.

THE figure of Constantine is one that has possibly been glorified unduly in the history of the Church. He had long been spoken of in glowing terms as the "first Christian Emperor," converted in a miraculous fashion when he saw a cross of light appear in the heavens, bearing the inscription: "In this sign shalt thou conquer." The unrelenting study of the past hundred years, however, has set much of this aside. What remains is the picture of a man who was undoubtedly sincere in his acceptance of the Christian God and of Christ the Saviour. It has been questioned, however, just how much of a "Christian" he actually was beyond this. While his conversion may have been sincere, and while many of his official acts are stamped with Christian influence, it is possibly best to say that Constantine was "sincerely wrong." He never really grasped the fullness of Christianity, and that can mean only one thing: he was never a true Christian. No one can be a faithful disciple of Christ by accepting only half of what Christ and His Church teach.

Constantine may never have been a member of the Church at all; he postponed his baptism until the year 337, just shortly before he died. He took leave of this life in a devout enough fashion, pledging himself to the life of a baptized Christian, and begging God's mercy for his sins. But it was not a Catholic who baptized him, but an Arian — no less than Eusebius of Nicomedia himself; his faith may have been the same. Despite his interest in the Council of Nicea, there were other less Christian aspects of Constantine's life. Among them must be included the murder he arranged of his wife, Fausta, and of one of his own sons, Crispus.

The greatest difficulty, however, was derived from Constantine's concept of the "Christian" emperor. He looked upon himself as the defender of the faith, but the faith he would defend was quite dependent upon his mood and his current advisers. In this way it came about that some time after Nicea, Constantine changed and became the defender of the Arians. It was he who was responsible for expelling Athanasius from his diocese the first time.

In history, whenever the political power has come to the defense of Christianity by involving itself in the operation of the Church, it has almost always ended by doing more harm to the Church than good. This is surely the case in the post-Nicean era. Arianism was not only to remain a vital heretical movement, but it was to make great progress; and this progress was to be due in large measure to the patronage of the Roman emperors.

When the bishops signed the Creed at Nicea, there was outwardly a great unanimity. But the sincerity of some of the bishops is surely open to question. A number evidently signed more at the insistence of Hosius and the Emperor than because of personal conviction; this was especially true of the Arian bishops — Eusebius above all.

Even among the Catholics who accepted the teaching in its entirety there was not a wholehearted agreement that all was well. There were those who still felt that the definition of a doctrine in nonscriptural terms was not well advised. They tended to look upon it as an innovation, the result of the pressure of a "liberal" group of some sort, intent upon destroying the faith of Scripture rather than defending it. This hesitancy opened the road for vacillation, and it helps explain the lapse, later on, even of some of the more devout and orthodox bishops.

There were two particular problems associated with the use of the "new" word, *homo-ousion;* both the Arians and the scriptural-minded Catholics realized this. There was, first of all, the fact that it is a term obviously influenced by the West, and even at this date such a state of affairs was not looked upon happily by many Eastern bishops. Tertullian had apparently introduced the word *consubstantialis* into the Latin vocabulary about the beginning of the third century. The fact that the Greek translation of such a term did find its way into the Nicean Creed is not unimportant; the overwhelming majority of the bishops present had come from the East. This fact alone emphasizes the influence of the West as well as the extreme usefulness of the term. Apparently it was Hosius who was most influential in securing its adoption by the Council, and he came from Spain.

Nevertheless, the word was somewhat new to the East, even though Origen and his disciples had used it. While the meaning intended at Nicea was clear, the fact that it was something of an innovation continued to disturb some souls. Moreover, the problem was further complicated by the fact that the very same word had been used to indicate something *different* in other Greek writers. The most outstanding instance was that of Paul of Samosata. He had used the word *homo-ousion* to indicate the exact opposite teaching. For him, to say that the Father and the Son are *homo-ousion* did not mean that the two divine Persons possessed the same divine nature. As he used it, the word meant that the "Father" and "Son" are simply two different names for the one God — the one and only divine Person. With this meaning in mind, Paul of Samosata had taught that the "Father" and "Son" are *homo-ousion* — that is, they are entirely identical and are not distinct persons at all. As a result, the local synod of Antioch had condemned Paul of Samosata in 268 for teaching that the Father and Son are *homo-ousion!*

Such a state of affairs could not help but breed further confusion in the East, even after the Nicean Creed had been issued. The Arians used these arguments in order to promote their teaching; they probably did so in some instances with malice aforethought. But even the more orthodox believers were led into confusion. After all, they recognized that Paul of Samosata had been condemned for saying that the Father and the Son were *homo-ousion,* and yet Nicea had explicitly decreed that they *are homo-ousion!*

Added to these technical problems, there came the politically ambitious schemes of the emperors and a number of the bishops. Arianism was, for some, a steppingstone to power, and they were quick to make use of it. They valued power and position far above orthodoxy in faith. Among these, it would seem that Eusebius of Nicomedia would take first place. He was interested above all in "getting ahead." He was little concerned with doctrinal precision, and would gladly have settled for a more vague statement at Nicea. He apparently did sign the Nicean Creed simply to keep his position at the time.

Shortly after Nicea, Eusebius somehow managed to convey this impression to the Emperor Constantine and was promptly exiled. Constantine died, however, in 337 and the empire had to find a new ruler. There was no difficulty in getting men who were willing to assume the burden; quite the opposite, there were far too many claiming the right to do so. The three sons of Constantine eventually emerged triumphant. At first they divided the vast empire three ways, but when one of them —

Constantine II — died three years later in a civil war with his brother, the authority rested with the remaining two: Constans and Constantius II.

The change in regime marked a new chapter in the history of the Councils. Actually it had already gotten under way in 330 when Constantine permitted Eusebius and Arius to return from exile. Eusebius and his followers at once went into action. Since they could not risk an open attack, they resorted to intrigues.

The technique adopted was very simple; it was used first of all on one who by now was their great enemy: Athanasius, the bishop of Alexandria. The technique consisted in managing somehow or other to place the orthodox bishop in disfavor, and then in installing an Arian bishop in his see, once he had been exiled. The case of Athanasius was a pattern of many to follow.

St. Athanasius had attended the Council of Nicea as a deacon and secretary to the old bishop of Alexandria who had first of all condemned Arius. By 328, however, Athanasius had succeeded the older man as head of the church at Alexandria. Upon his return from exile, Eusebius first directed his attention to Athanasius, managing to maneuver him into disfavor with Constantine. As a result, in 335 Athanasius was sent into exile by the Emperor.

With Athanasius out of the way, and Eusebius back in power with Constantine as his special patron, it seemed sure that the Arians — or the *Eusebians,* as they are also known — were sure to triumph. One thing still remained undone: Arius himself had not yet been received back into the Church, although recalled from exile. Constantine finally decreed that this be done by the bishop of Constantinople (since public resentment still made it impossible at Alexandria). At that very moment, however, Arius died (336), and soon afterward Constantine also passed on. The triumph was incomplete.

When the sons of Constantine took over the rule of the empire,

Athanasius was allowed to return; thus the two opponents were free to carry on the dispute. The battle continued mostly by way of intrigue, however. Of the two remaining sons of Constantine, Constans was a baptized Catholic, while Constantius II favored Eusebius. Constans was not a particularly healthy man, but he was the more powerful of the two. As a result, until his death in 350, his presence warded off any Arian attack on the West and at least limited greatly any violence in the East.

After the death of Constantine the Great, however, the conflict had become increasingly evident. Eusebius had soon managed to have himself appointed bishop of Constantinople. It was an office of tremendous importance, and it placed him in a position to do much to further the Arian interests.

The technique continued, then, of attempting to fill the various dioceses with Arian bishops. The first big attempt was to replace the recently returned Athanasius with an Arian bishop in Alexandria. To this was added a second technique, one that was to become even more important in later years. It consisted of inserting synonyms into the decrees of the Councils, thus giving them a completely different meaning but with very little outward change in wording.

There were also appeals to Rome from both sides, a number of local synods, and threatening statements on the part of the Emperor. The whole Christian world seemed torn in doctrinal conflict. Today, historians will place descriptive tags on various groups — a practice complicated by the Greek words used for this purpose. The names are based on the solution the group proposed. Four large groups can be distinguished, one Catholic and three Arian:

1. The *Homo-ousions*, led by Athanasius, who insisted on the full meaning of Nicea: Christ is of the one and same substance as the Father.

2. The *Anomoeans*. These were a group of Arians who, after

Nicea, came out into the open and clearly stated in express terms what others had said more indirectly. They claimed, therefore, that the Word (the *Logos*) was entirely *unlike* the Father. Hence the name, from the Greek word *a-homoios*. The *a* stands for "not"; and the adjective *homoios* means "like." Thus the Word is "not like" the Father. They represent the teaching that is exactly the opposite of that of Nicea. (They are also called *Eunomeans* from the name of one of their leaders, Eunomius.)

3. The *Homoeans*. This group is named by using only the Greek adjective *homoios* (which means "like" or "similar"). They were a vague group who hoped that the entire debate could be solved by side-stepping the issue. They proposed that we hold that the Word was "like" the Father, dropping the *ousia* (substance) of Nicea entirely. In this way, a type of compromise peace would result; the Arians could understand the phrase in their own way, the Catholics in theirs. Since their motives in suggesting this are recognized as more political than doctrinal, they are also known as the *Politicals*.

4. The *Homoi-ousions*. This was the largest of all the Arian groups after Nicea; they are generally known today as the *Semi-Arians*. Their solution involved a departure from Nicea, but they attempted to make the change as easy as possible. All they did was change the adjective *homos* (the "same") to *homoios* ("like" or "similar"). They added it, however, to the *ousia* ("substance") used at Nicea. In this way, there was little change. The *homo-ousion* of Nicea became simply *homoi-ousion*. The only apparent difference was this extra "i" (a *iota* in the Greek alphabet). But the meaning was completely changed. If the *Logos* was only "similar" in substance, He would still not be true God.

These many divisions resulted in great confusion on all sides. Smaller councils or synods were held at various places, but none of them came up with a lasting solution. Pope Liberius (352–

366) had suggested a Council, for example, and the Emperor Constantius agreed, but whatever meetings were held only ended in even greater confusion. At some of them the Arians turned to strong-arm tactics; the decrees issued were simply heretical. Meeting after meeting ended in this fashion. About the most noteworthy result in each case was either sending St. Athanasius into exile or recalling him — depending upon which party won the upper hand. Athanasius was, by now, the leading defender of the faith of Nicea; hence his importance as a symbol of the entire debate.

The whole question now centered about the Nicean Creed: Should it be accepted or not? At one gathering at Milan the Arian bishops became so enraged that they dragged the pen from the hand of the bishop of Milan as he was about to sign the Creed; a veritable riot resulted. The Emperor finally intervened and forced the bishops to condemn Athanasius, to reject Nicea, and receive the Arians into full union in the Church!

In the midst of this seemingly endless confusion, even Pope Liberius was tricked into a difficult position. He still remains one of the most discussed men of the period. Liberius continued to insist upon a free Council, but his wishes were not heeded. Instead, there came forth from Sirmium (the villa of the imperial court) one formula after another, more or less Arian in tone. The first such formula had passed over the word *homoousion* entirely; the second was an obvious Arian decree, an open denial of Nicea; and the third was something of a compromise, but, understood in proper fashion, it could be viewed as in agreement with Nicea.

The signature of Liberius was needed, of course, to give real force to these formulas, and to this day historians debate whether Liberius signed any of the formulas, and if so which one he did sign. Whatever did take place, it is certain enough that Liberius was, in point of fact, a stanch defender of Nicea (and also of

Athanasius, which then meant the same thing). If he signed any, it would seem that it was the third formula, which admits of a proper interpretation; if he signed the second, however, it is clear from his other actions that he was tricked into it.

In any event, it raises no special problem in regard to papal infallibility, since Liberius never clearly issued a solemn statement on his own authority. He preferred to continue demanding a free Council, with no interference from the Emperor. For this he was rewarded with exile himself! Liberius was kidnaped by night at the order of the Emperor and carried off to the imperial court. It seemed as though the Arians were in complete control. Those bishops who refused to condemn Athanasius were removed from their sees; even the Pope was now held captive.

Nothing was settled, however, since the group in favor with the Emperor changed from the Semi-Arians to the Anomoeans to the Politicals and back again. Things continued in this manner until Constantius died in 361. The immediate successors of Constantius came and went rapidly. In 379, Theodosius became the emperor in the East, and out of all this confusion rose the first Council of Constantinople (381).

By this time, Athanasius had died (373) and the leadership of the Catholic party had passed first to St. Basil and then to St. Gregory Nazianzen. Yet when Theodosius came to power, the Arians dominated everywhere in the East, especially at Constantinople; the orthodox believers in that city had neither bishop nor church. The new Emperor, however, was a devout Catholic and he wished to change all that. He decided, therefore, to restore the Catholics to power and to expel the Arians. To secure a lasting peace, he finally convoked the free Council that had been sought twenty or thirty years before by Pope Liberius. In this way the State broke officially with Arianism, and for the first time in years expressed in a clear fashion its acceptance of the Nicean faith.

I Constantinople

Of all the General Councils, I Constantinople is, for a number of reasons, one of the most perplexing. Considering the futile attempts of the past, it did not seem that this Council would effect much more than these earlier gatherings had done; nevertheless it did, and the power of the Holy Spirit triumphed. It is unique in the history of the Councils. From all appearances, only the bishops of the East were invited. About 186 bishops took part, but not a single one from the west. Despite the frequent requests of Pope Liberius and his successors for a free Council, it seems that now not even Pope Damasus (366–384) was contacted in regard to this gathering; he did not take part in the proceedings, not even through his legates. We would have to conclude, in fact, that the Council was formally "convoked" by the Roman Pontiff at a much later date; history is silent on any approval given by Damasus I. In the sixth century, however, I Constantinople is listed in the papal decrees among the other General Councils of the fourth and fifth centuries.

We have very little information concerning what took place at this Council. It opened in May of 381; it most probably closed in July of that year. There were in all three men who presided over the sessions: Meletius, Gregory of Nazianzen, and finally Nectarius. One of the first tasks was the election of a new bishop of Constantinople; the Arian bishop chose to leave the city rather than comply. For this office St. Gregory Nazianzen was chosen.

The bishops then turned to the doctrinal questions of Arianism. About thirty-six Arian bishops had accepted the invitation to attend the Council, but, since they all refused to accept the Nicean Creed, they had left the city before the Council began. The bishops were especially concerned with a group of Semi-Arians who had fallen into error in regard to the Holy Spirit; this new error had to be condemned as well. Just as the Arians had claimed that the Word was only a creature and not God, so these Semi-Arians stated the same thing about the Holy Spirit. They are called *Macedonians* from one of their chief leaders, Macedonius (who had been the bishop of Constantinople about twenty years earlier).

When the thirty-six Arian bishops left the city, the remaining 150 went on to reaffirm the faith of Nicea. After all these years of dispute, they simply repeated the *homo-ousion* of Nicea, adding nothing more. The formula they issued seems to have been a Jerusalem Creed, completed by the formula of Nicea; the Council simply made this formula its own. Because of the teaching of the Macedonians, this Creed includes a more definite statement concerning the Catholic belief in the Holy Spirit: "We believe in the Holy Spirit, the Lord, the Giver of life; he proceeds from the Father, is adored and honored together with the Father and the Son; he spoke through the prophets." With certain smaller changes, it is this Creed that we recite in the liturgy of the Mass today.

In this way, the doctrinal quarrel was finally settled; the faith of Nicea on this point was once again secure. New troubles would arise, but they would be of a slightly different nature. One source of difficulty, however, was created by the third canon formulated by I Constantinople: "The bishop of Constantinople shall hold the first rank after the bishop of Rome, because Constantinople is New Rome." In this lay the seeds of discord and political unrest that would eventually lead to the great schism of the Eastern Churches. But that is another story, to which we must return later on; there are other doctrinal problems that must be treated first.

CHAPTER V ... *Council of Ephesus*

AFTER I Constantinople, the divinity of the Word was well secured in the Church. The picture changed somewhat at this point. The earlier debates had centered around the Trinity, and the question was asked: "What is the relationship of the *Logos* (Word) to the Father?" It indicated a special concern for Christ in His *divine* nature and His relationship to the Trinity.

In the fifth century, we can note a new interest, although the debates and crises continue to mount on all sides. Those now taking part in the discussions all admitted the fact that the *Logos* is truly God in the sense defined at Nicea. They began to inquire about the relationship of the *Logos* to the *human* nature of Christ. The big question now became: "What is the relationship of the *Logos* (Word) to Jesus of Nazareth?"

While the controversy was being waged between the Arians and the Catholics toward the end of the fourth century, a new outlook was being developed. The Catholics had been insisting that Christ was both true God and true man. The Arians had really ended up by stating the exact opposite: Christ was neither true God nor true man. He was not of the same substance with the Father, hence He was not God; but the *Logos* was also a superangelic being, created before all other creatures, so that the Arians tended to pass over the humanity of Christ.

In the back of this Arian teaching there was the seed of another error. This started to come to light especially in the teaching of Apollinaris; his error had also been condemned at I Constantinople in 381: *Apollinarianism.*

Apollinaris was the bishop of Laodicea in Syria, and a violent anti-Arian. But in opposing that doctrine he himself fell into another extreme. Apollinaris accepted the divinity of Christ in the full and orthodox sense, but he failed to do full justice to His humanity. Thus, differing from the Catholics and from the Arians, Apollinaris would say that Christ was true God, but not true man.

The reason for this position was more or less his acceptance of Plato's philosophy, which he then applied wrongly to Christ. Plato, a Greek philosopher who died about 347 B.C., had spoken of a threefold division in man: he had a body, a soul, and a spirit. The "spirit" was the element in man that made it possible for him to think, to act as a rational human being. The soul simply joined with the body to give it life; it is what he would call a "sensitive soul," rather than a rational soul.

When Apollinaris spoke of Christ, therefore, he claimed that Christ was a true human being in the sense that He did have a soul; but this was a sensitive soul only. Thus Christ had a true body and the five senses; He had true human feelings and emotions. All this pertained to the sense life.

In regard to the "spirit," however, which Apollinaris considered the source of intellectual life, he held that Christ had no such spirit: He possessed, in other words, no rational soul. For Apollinaris, the *Logos* took over the role of the "spirit" in Christ, and was therefore the source of His thought life and the acts of His will.

Since man is a combination of body and soul, to be a true

man means to *think* and to *will* to do things in the very same manner that other human beings think and will. Apollinaris failed to explain properly the humanity of Christ for this reason. If Christ had no human "spirit," He also had no human thoughts, no human will; thus He could not be human in the same way that other men are. And if this were true, then what is to be said of those texts in Scripture which say that Christ "prayed" to the Father in heaven, and that He "obeyed" the command of the Father in dying upon the cross? These are actions of a *human* mind and a *human* will. Christ could not pray or obey insofar as He is the second Person of the Trinity; this He could do only insofar as He is man and possesses a true human intellect and will.

This, then, was the starting point for all the debates of the next two or three centuries. It was to lead to a fuller understanding of Christ, and when the debates had ended, there would be a record of four more General Councils that had arisen to clarify these questions.

Apollinaris had really intended only to defend the unity of Christ. He had wanted to show that Christ the Man was really and truly the *Logos*, the second Person of the Trinity. To him it seemed best, therefore, to explain *all* the mental activities of Christ by considering them the actions of the *Logos*. In doing this, however, he was really teaching that Christ was not a true man at all; He possessed no true human nature. It was only to be expected that he would soon be attacked.

His greatest opposition came from the school of Antioch. Diodore of Tarsus opposed him at once, laying much greater emphasis on the two realities in Christ: a true and perfect human nature as well as a true and perfect divine nature. He passed this teaching on to Theodore of Mopsuestia, and Theodore, in turn, may have been the teacher who passed it on to Nestorius. At any rate, when we come to Nestorius we find a man who is thoroughly penetrated by the principles of the school of Antioch. It is after this man that the second great heresy of the early Church is named: *Nestorianism.* This heresy was concerned with the relationship of Christ's human nature to His divine nature.

In his own eyes at least, Nestorius was a great defender of the faith. He was strongly opposed to the Arians and the Semi-Arians who had already been condemned. With the teachings of the school of Antioch as his norm, however, he went a step further. He thought that he could perceive within the Church itself another error that concerned Christ, and he struck out against it.

Like Theodore of Mopsuestia, Nestorius was far from achieving any great clarity in the statement of his position. While the underlying principles may have been obscure, the final conclusions were not. For this reason, Nestorius soon aroused the ire of the bishops of his time because of his teaching, which failed to do justice to Catholic faith. Theodore had emphasized so much the fact that Christ was both God and man (against Apollinaris and his followers), that he practically ended up by talking about two entirely distinct persons: Christ, who was God; and Jesus of Nazareth, who was man. Nestorius did the same, even more clearly.

Nestorius saw a further application of this position which he made his own in a special way. He concluded that Mary brought forth only Jesus, and not the *Logos.* The *Logos* only began to dwell in a special manner in Jesus of Nazareth some time after He was born. This meant, therefore, that we are not justified in calling Mary the "Mother of God," except in some loose, figurative sense. She was only the Mother of Christ, in whom God (the *Logos*) later came to dwell. It was in this conclusion about Mary that the error of Nestorius became most apparent.

When Nestorius became the bishop of Constantinople, a new crisis was in the process of formation. About the year 428, one of his disciples, the monk Anastasius, mentioned this point in a sermon; the clergy and the faithful were shocked. When they complained of it to the bishop, Nestorius not only refused to condemn the teaching, but he made use of the opportunity to set forth the doctrine himself.

For many years now, the faithful had spoken of the Blessed Mother as the *Theotokos* — the "Mother of God." There are indications of its use in prayers as early as the third century. Nestorius now claimed that this was a dangerous word. He held that we ought to speak of Mary only as the *Christotokos* — the "Mother of Christ." Thus the defense of the true doctrine concerning Christ was necessarily linked so intimately to the honor given to Mary as His Mother. One cannot dishonor Mary without dishonoring Christ as well, and those who heard Nestorius preach realized this.

The Catholic faith has always insisted that Christ possesses two complete and perfect natures, the human and the divine. These two natures are not in any way confused with one another; there is nothing essential lacking to either. As Scripture indicates, Christ is true God and true Man.

These two natures are united, however, insofar as they belong to one and the same Person: the second Person of the Trinity. From all eternity this divine Person possessed His divine nature. Without losing this, He also assumed, at the time of the Incarnation, a human nature that was fashioned in the body of Mary. He made entirely His own this human body and the spiritual soul God infused into it; this was accomplished by the action of the entire Trinity. It is accordingly the human body and soul of that Person to whom the Trinity united it: the second Person of the Trinity.

Since it is through the *Person* that the human and divine in

Christ are united, the Church speaks of the "hypostatic union" — a word derived from the Greek word for person (*hypostasis*). It means that in the union of the human and divine natures, both natures remain complete and perfect; they are united, however, "in the person" (*hypostasis*) of the divine Word, the second Person of the Trinity.

Nestorius, on the other hand, seemed to hold that there was originally a "human person" resulting from the union of this body and soul in Christ (just as there was a "divine Person" in the Trinity — the second Person, the *Logos*). Nestorius indicated that some kind of *new* person resulted from the union of these two. He did not hold that this human person and the divine Person were either fused together or destroyed, as later heretics did; but they were joined together in such a way that the human person was somehow subordinate to the divine person.

No matter how you understand this, however, it can only amount to saying that there is no more than a "moral union" of two entirely distinct persons in Christ. The so-called human person is "more or less" joined to the divine Person, but that is all. The end result is that when you consider the body and soul of Jesus, the Son of Mary, you do not really consider the body and soul of *God*. The *Logos* only dwells *in* this body and soul, as in a temple. The body and soul really belong to the "human person."

For Nestorius, then, Jesus of Nazareth is simply the "God-bearer," and not really God. Since the *Logos* dwells within Him, Nestorius would say that Jesus is "one" with God, but not in the sense that the Church had always understood it. This became most clear in the further conclusion regarding the Blessed Virgin. According to Nestorius, Mary was, we might say, the Mother of the "temple," but not of the *Logos;* she was not the Mother of God, but only the Mother of Jesus of Nazareth.

On the other hand, the Church insisted that a mother is always the mother of a *person;* she is not simply the producer of a body. Common sense alone indicates this. A mother is mother of some- one, not something. Ultimately the question, therefore, is this: "Precisely who is Christ?" If Christ is God, then Mary is the Mother of God, the mother of the divine Person. If Christ is not a human person, Mary cannot be the mother of a human person.

Mary is not the Mother of God in His *divine* nature, obviously; God is eternal, infinite. But in becoming the Mother of God in His *human* nature, she was necessarily the Mother of the Person to whom that human nature belonged, and that Person was the second Person of the Trinity. This was the chief point of the entire dispute. To call Mary the Mother of God is really another way of saying that Christ is God: one divine Person with both a human and a divine nature.

Nestorius was most firm in his position. He excommunicated the members of his own church who refused to accept his teach- ing. Some appealed at once to the Emperor, while others notified the Bishop of Rome. In this way the stage was set for the third General Council, the Council of Ephesus in 431.

From Rome there came the request of Pope Celestine I (422– 432) for further information about the dispute at Constantinople. He wrote to the patriarch of Alexandria, St. Cyril, for this in- formation. Thus Cyril became the leading character of this de- bate, somewhat as Athanasius had been in regard to the Arians.

Cyril sent his report to Rome with the deacon, Posidonius; he reached there in the spring of 430. The Western bishops ex- amined the teaching of Nestorius at Rome and declared that it was heretical. The Pope then sent word to Cyril that he was to depose Nestorius if he did not reject his teaching within ten days after he heard their decision.

Before proceeding with this directive, however, Cyril decided to call together the bishops of the East at Alexandria in order to investigate again the precise error of Nestorius. Perhaps more than the Western bishops, Cyril may have realized the danger of not pinning Nestorius down to precise points; the long and troublesome history of the Arian controversy was still fresh enough in the memory of the East.

The Eastern bishops gathered together, and on November 3, 430, they issued a letter along with the famous twelve *Anathemata* of Cyril. These were a series of propositions condemning errors about Christ. Nestorius was to subscribe to them or be deposed. They were intended to be very precise doctrinal statements, eliminating all possibility of misunderstanding. As it happened, they were phrased in Cyril's own words, and there was some possibility of misunderstanding; they were destined to play a role in later history.

Nestorius and his followers rejected the entire idea, and turned to accuse Cyril himself of being a heretic. A number of other bishops also supported Nestorius, above all John, the patriarch of Antioch. Some did so because they were in agreement with Nestorius' position; others were perhaps confused by the terminology of Cyril. But the battle was on again.

The Roman emperors then took the next step. The empire was still divided between two men: Theodosius II was the Eastern emperor, and Valentinian III was the emperor in the West — the last really effective one of the West. Theodosius, however, was the moving force in this matter. Although neither Pope Celestine nor Cyril had asked for a Council, the question had been mentioned; Nestorius especially had sought a Council. Theodosius therefore convoked a Council that was to open on Pentecost Sunday of 431 at Ephesus. This was a famous seaport along the Aegean Sea, a city known in pagan times for its devotion to the Greek goddess, Diana. In Christian Ephesus a far more noble woman had taken the place of Diana in their hearts: the Mother of God. It was only fitting that her glories should happen to be extolled there at this third Ecumenical Council.

The Pope had known of the desire of Nestorius and others for a Council; hence there was no great surprise at Rome. He agreed to send three legates to represent him at the gathering: two bishops, Arcadius and Projectus, and the priest, Philip. They were given careful instructions. First of all, they were to attach themselves firmly to Cyril of Alexandria, who would serve as their guide.

Second, they were to safeguard the rights of the Bishop of Rome. They were to come as judges, not as parties to a controversy. The Bishop of Rome had already settled the question of Nestorius and his teaching; they were simply to make sure that this was carried out. Owing to this directive the Council produced some of the most outstanding testimony of that century to the Roman primacy, since the bishops gave vocal expression to their acceptance of papal authority.

Lastly, considering the difficulty of travel in those days, the legates were told that, should they arrive late, they were to investigate carefully everything that had taken place before their arrival. As time would prove, this was a bit of advice well given.

When the Council opened, most of the bishops present were, once again, from the East. Africa sent one deacon; at the time it was sorely pressed with attacks from the Vandals and not many could attend the Council; the same was true in Italy, which sent only the legates of the Pope. There was a great deal of difficulty involved in getting there on time. When the appointed day arrived, the papal legates had not yet arrived, and the patriarch of Antioch, John (who had been appointed by the Emperor to preside), was also absent. In John's case the delay may have been on purpose. He was a friend of Nestorius, and may not have wished to take part in the condemnation; at any rate, he did send on word that they ought not wait too long, should he be delayed.

After waiting sixteen days, Cyril insisted that they go on with the Council; thus the first session actually got under way on June 22, 431. Nestorius was there with six bishops; Cyril with about 50 bishops; and Memnon, the bishop of Ephesus, was present with about 40 of his suffragan bishops and 12 from Pamphylia. At the start there were about 159 bishops who attended the Council, although 198 signatures appear on the final condemnation. Count Candidian was present as the representative of the Emperor.

All went well that first day. The Council opened in the Church of St. Mary at Ephesus. Nestorius was offered an opportunity to appear three times, but refused. The letters of Cyril and of Pope Celestine, in which the teaching of Nestorius was condemned, were read and approved. A number of other statements taken from the writings of earlier Fathers were also read; these were offered in support of the teaching of Celestine and Cyril. Nestorius was then declared to be deposed as bishop of Constantinople and excommunicated for his heretical teaching.

The people of Ephesus celebrated this great triumph that very night. They passed through the lighted city, carrying torches and incense in honor of what had been accomplished. The truth concerning Christ and the honor due His Mother had once again been affirmed.

But this was not the end. As with many of the other Councils, a storm was yet to arise. The next day the Council officially notified Nestorius of the sentence; word was also sent to the priests of Constantinople, informing them that their bishop had been deposed. Nestorius was angered; so also was Candidian, the representative of the Emperor. Candidian had opposed the holding of a session until the others arrived. In the name of the Emperor, therefore, Candidian promptly declared the entire proceedings null and void.

A few days later, John, the patriarch of Antioch, arrived and showed himself no less receptive to what had been done. He sided with Candidian, and gathered together with 43 bishops to form a rebel council. They at once issued their own decrees, deposing Cyril and Memnon (the bishop of Ephesus), and excommunicating their followers. They claimed that they, and not Nestorius, were the real heretics, guilty of Arianism and Apollinarianism.

The Emperor was quite upset by this turn of events and demanded that the bishops all remain in Ephesus until an investigation could be made. About July 10, the papal legates finally arrived, and set things in order. Following the directives of Pope Celestine, they reviewed all that had been done. When the acts had all been read, they approved and added their signatures to the decrees. They then notified the Emperor that the East and the West were in accord, and demanded permission to elect a new bishop of Constantinople.

There were in all six more sessions from July 10 to August 31. In these sessions the decrees against Cyril and Memnon were declared invalid. John of Antioch and his party, however, refused to agree to the proceedings. This was to remain a problem even after the Council.

A number of other decrees were also issued, concerning above all the heresy of Pelagius which had been upsetting the West in particular during these same years; this had been one of the chief concerns of the great St. Augustine. He had died in 430, but had been sent an invitation to attend the Council of Ephesus; those concerned had not as yet heard of his death. Another decree pronounced that no one could add anything to the Creed issued at Nicea. This also was destined to play a role in the later disputes at the time of the Great Eastern Schism. But the chief work was the condemnation of the error of Nestorius.

When all was finished, the work of Ephesus was essentially a triumph. Nestorianism was doomed. It marked the beginning, however, of further complications. The Emperor Theodosius II officially ended the council toward the end of October, 431. Strangely, he had accepted both the condemnation of Nestorius by the authentic Council and the condemnation of Cyril by the rebel council. Cyril, however, was able to gain the approval of the Emperor, and through the help of his friends, Theodosius gave way. In October of 431, the Emperor permitted Cyril to return to Egypt as the bishop of Alexandria; he continued to recognize the condemnation of Nestorius.

Nevertheless, John of Antioch and his followers still exercised their influence. A division had resulted from the Council, and this had to be healed. Neither the Pope nor the Emperor accepted the condemnation of John of Antioch and his party. By thus leaving the door open for a peaceful solution, much good resulted. By 433, the followers of Cyril and John of Antioch had discussed the questions and assured one another that they both held to the same doctrine, even though their terminology might differ. All signed the formula of agreement, and the matter rested, for the time being at least. Ephesus had won over all of those concerned.

CHAPTER VI ... *Council of Chalcedon*

The intervention of Cyril of Alexandria at Ephesus had been tremendously important in defending the faith against Nestorius. Cyril, however, was a man who spoke and wrote in a terminology that could be misleading; this was the big problem that had disturbed John of Antioch. For one thing, Cyril had often spoken of Christ by referring to the "one incarnate nature of God the Word." To Cyril this indicated especially that there was but "one person" in Christ. Others understood it to mean but "one nature." As a result, Cyril finally set this phrase aside, and accepted the phrase of Antioch: "the union of two natures."

This approach, however, was going to have its effect in what follows. While Cyril wished to affirm the traditional faith of the Church, the phrase he had used could be taken to indicate something entirely different. As long as Cyril was alive, such confusion could be avoided. But, in 444, he died. John of Antioch had already died, as well as Pope Sixtus, who had reigned at the time of the agreement of 433. By the year 448, therefore, a new crisis was upon the Church, new debates, a new heresy, and eventually a new Council.

The ordinary catechism today will tell us that Christ is the second "Person" of the Trinity, and that in addition to His divine "nature" He assumed a human "nature" in order to save mankind. The words "nature" and "person" are technical terms that have come to indicate something very definite in Catholic teaching. Many years elapsed however, before everyone agreed upon what precise word to use to express these ideas. In fact, much of the difficulty in the centuries we are talking about arose from the unsettled terminology. What made matters even worse, men not only used different Greek or Latin words when speaking about "nature" and "person," but they sometimes used the *same* word to mean both things.

There are instances, for example, when the Greek word generally used for person (*hypostasis*) was used by some men to mean "nature." The same was true of other important terms. There were no dictionaries to solve the problem; a dictionary has to wait until men agree on the meaning of a certain word. This, of course, invited great confusion, and only with the solemn definitions of the great Councils were the problems finally solved.

When we speak of "nature" we are concerned with exactly what makes something what it is. Nature is the answer to the question "What is it?" Whatever goes to make a human being a human being (and not a flower or animal) is his "nature." In this way we can distinguish between inanimate nature (like rocks), plant nature, animal nature, human nature, angelic nature, and divine nature — right up the scale.

On the other hand, "person" is the answer to the question "Who is it?" We never speak of persons, then, except with the last three classes: men, angels, God. That is why we will not point to a dog and ask "Who is that?" To be a person, one must have a mind. If one cannot think or if one does not at least have the basic *power* of thinking, he is not a person. A baby, therefore, or a mentally retarded individual is truly a person, since he does have that power, even though the use of it is hindered for some reason. This intellectual power makes it possible for a person to "act" as an intelligent being, and to be responsible for what he does.

In Christ, therefore, there is only one "person" — one who acts, who is responsible for whatever is done either in His divine nature or in His human nature. Thus we can truly say that "God died upon the cross," because it is a *person* who dies. When the human nature of Christ died it was God *in His human nature* (although not in His divine nature) who died.

This problem became the subject of special debate after the Council of Ephesus. Nestorius had tended to speak of two "persons" in regard to Christ: a divine and eternal Person, and a human person. Those who opposed him naturally wanted to stress the fact that there is only one person in Christ. Whether He acted as God (in His divine nature) or as man (in His human nature), it was always God, the second Person of the Trinity who did these things.

In stressing this truth, however, some men went to the opposite extreme. Offering the phrase of St. Cyril as their defense, they claimed that there was not only one Person, but also only one nature in Christ. Cyril had spoken of "one incarnate nature (*physis*) of God the Word." For Cyril, the word *physis* meant "person"; for these others, however, it meant "nature." The result was a new heresy known as the Monophysite heresy. (It comes from the Greek words, *mono,* which means "one"; and *physis,* meaning "nature.") It is also known as *Eutychianism,* from the name of its chief defendant, Eutyches, abbot of a monastery near Constantinople.

In addition to Eutyches, three other men play a large role in the history of this controversy: Pope Leo the Great; Flavian, the bishop of Constantinople; and the Emperor Marcian. The name of Leo in the middle of the fifth century was to be forever associated with the triumph of the Council of Chalcedon;

Flavian was to work in close association with Leo; and Marcian was the one who insisted on the Council.

The abbot Eutyches was greatly upset by Nestorianism, so much so that he saw signs of it everywhere he looked. His reaction was the opposite extreme. In emphasizing the oneness and unity of Christ, he really *destroyed* the two natures. What resulted from his teaching was something new — a kind of "mixture" of the human and the divine, in which the human was absorbed, as it were, by the divine. Other Monophysites would vary the teaching so that the divinity disappeared in the humanity, or was changed into the human nature. But the end result in every case was only *one nature*. The example used by Eutyches has become famous: "As a drop of milk let fall into the ocean is quickly absorbed, so also was the human nature of Christ entirely absorbed by the Divinity."

Among those to oppose Eutyches was Theodoret, the bishop of Cyrrhus, his greatest opponent. He was the man who, so to speak, had taken over the leadership of the orthodox believers when Cyril of Alexandria died in 444. He was not the great mind that Cyril had been, but he was a more precise and exact theologian. Thus he was able to clear up some of the misunderstandings caused by the terminology of Cyril.

On the other hand, Eutyches did more than disturb others; he took the initiative and set out to attack them. One of those toward whom he directed his wrath was Eusebius, the bishop of Dorylaeum; Eutyches was certain that this man was teaching heresy. As a rule, Eutyches was quite secure and able to achieve his goals. He was a powerful and influential man; as his patron he had the rather sinister patriarch of Alexandria, Dioscoros. Eusebius, however, was not afraid of Eutyches in any way. He promptly denounced him to Flavian, the bishop of Constantinople.

Flavian may well have feared Eutyches; when he was openly

denounced, however, Flavian had to act. He summoned Eutyches to a synod at Constantinople in 448; after several refusals, Eutyches appeared, guarded by the soldiers of the Emperor Theodosius II (who had taken kindly to Eutyches and his followers). Eutyches refused to retract his teaching, and insisted all the more that there are not two natures in Christ, but only one. Flavian's council of bishops at once deposed him from his office as abbot and excommunicated him from the Church.

The scene next shifted to Rome. The Emperor had appealed to Pope Leo on behalf of Eutyches. At the same time, Eutyches' special patron, Dioscoros, went into action at Alexandria, and declared that the sentences passed on Eutyches were null and void. Finding such favor from those in high positions, Eutyches asked the Emperor to convoke a Council and it was agreed; a Council was to open in August of 449 at Ephesus.

Fortunately the Roman Pontiff at the time was truly one of the "great" men of history, as his name indicates. Leo knew how to deal with people, and he was not inexperienced in the problems of diplomacy. Above all, he was a skilled theologian, well able to enter into this controversy. Eventually he had on hand the letter of Eutyches concerning the trial, the recommendation of the Emperor, and a report from Flavian.

Having considered the entire matter, Leo agreed to the Emperor's plan for a Council at Ephesus, and named three delegates to represent him. At the same time he wrote the famous letter to Flavian, expounding the true faith of the Church in regard to Christ; it is known as the "Dogmatic Epistle" of Leo the Great.

A short time later, on August 8, 449, the Council opened at Ephesus with about 130 bishops present. It took place in the same church where Nestorius had been condemned in 431, but it turned out to be a vastly different affair! The wily Dioscoros, patriarch of Alexandria, presided at the command of the Emperor Theodosius. He ignored the papal legates entirely, and refused to permit the reading of the "Epistle" from Leo. The Council then went on to do the exact opposite of what had been intended: it acquitted Eutyches and condemned Flavian, the bishop of Constantinople. Claiming that it was "Nestorian" to affirm two natures in Christ, the bishops once again took up the terminology of Cyril of Alexandria — understood, of course, in the sense held by the Monophysites. Theodoret of Cyrrhus was also deposed; and Flavian was so badly treated that he soon died.

The full report, however, finally reached Rome. Before he died, Flavian had sent an appeal, and Theodoret also wrote to Leo; and when the papal legates returned, Rome understood all. Leo gave to this gathering the name by which it has been known since: the "Robber Synod of Ephesus." In these proceedings, said Leo, we see no Council, but a den of thieves (*Latrocinium*). He at once declared invalid all that had been done. This was on October 6, 449. With the support of the Emperor, however, it did seem at the time as though the Monophysites had triumphed.

As had happened in the past, death was soon to intervene and change the entire picture. On July 28, 450, Theodosius, the emperor, died. His sister, Pulcheria, married a famous general of the time, Marcian; they became the new rulers. A devout couple, they set about correcting the evils. The orthodox bishops were recalled, Eutyches was sent away, and eventually the various bishops rejected the decrees of the "Robber Synod."

The suggestion was made of calling another Council, this time to proceed properly. Leo advised against it for various reasons. For one thing, matters were improving without open debate, and it seemed best to postpone such a General Council. Moreover, the barbarians were again attacking in the West, and it would be difficult for Western bishops to attend.

[60]

Before Leo's letter reached the East, however, steps had been taken by Marcian and Pulcheria to convoke the Council. It was to open at Nicea, this time, on September 1, 451. Again Leo agreed, and appointed other legates to represent him, giving them very precise instructions on what they were to do.

By a change in plans, the site was moved to another city, so that this Council did not become II Nicea. At the beginning of September about 500 bishops had gathered at Nicea, but the Emperor was busy fighting off the Vandals, and could not be there. The bishops continued their preparations, but grew tired of waiting. Marcian then asked them to transfer to a city nearer to Constantinople where he would be in closer touch with the Council, even though he did not attend. The spot chosen was Chalcedon, directly across from Constantinople (or Byzantium, at it was also known at that time).

The fourth General Council opened at Chalcedon on October 8, 451. It was closed officially on November 1 of that year, but its greatest work was accomplished by October 25, when the doctrinal decree was solemnly approved.

Of the first four Councils, Chalcedon stands out as by far the most important and glorious. It was attended by more bishops (about 600) than any of the previous gatherings. They came mostly from the East because of the difficulties with the barbarian invasions in the West. In addition to the papal legates, only two bishops from Africa were in attendance. The Eastern bishops, however, came from all over, and in great numbers.

This Council also stands out because of the profundity of the doctrinal decree, which is a superb summary of all that had been clarified concerning Christ and the Trinity during these first centuries; it also established firmly the terminology that has remained with the Church until this very day. In this way it completed the work of these earlier Councils. It seems, in a way, that the Church had to debate the two extremes of Nestorius and Eutyches in order to set forth in clear and technical language the doctrine received from the Apostles. In doing this, Chalcedon became the touchstone of doctrinal truth in this matter for all succeeding centuries.

The Council opened in the Church of the martyr, St. Euphemia. As with the Council of Ephesus, we possess far more in the way of records of what took place than we have from Nicea and I Constantinople. They have come to us both in Greek and Latin, since both languages had been used. There is still a question of precisely how many sessions took place. Some have said fourteen or fifteen; others twenty-one. The doctrinal problems were settled, however, in the first six.

The papal legates presided, although the representatives of the Emperor were also much in evidence; but they did not interfere with the work of the Council or the authority of the Roman Pontiff. In fact, apart from the doctrine concerning Christ, Chalcedon has left to the world the greatest testimony of an Eastern Council to the primacy of the Pope. At the end of the second session on October 10, after the reading of the "Dogmatic Epistle" of Pope Leo the Great, the bishops cried out: "Behold the faith of the fathers, the faith of the Apostles. . . . Thus through Leo has Peter spoken!"

One of the chief tasks of the Council, obviously, was to give a solution to the disciplinary problems that had arisen. In the course of the sessions, therefore, the acts of the "Robber Synod" were read; Flavian (now dead) and Eusebius (who had first denounced Eutyches) were declared innocent of the charges levied against them at Ephesus. The bishops who had been active at that illicit synod were then deposed, including Dioscoros of Alexandria. Eutyches, so roundly condemned by the Council, was finally sent into exile, along with his patron, Dioscoros; penalties were prescribed for those who insisted on remaining faithful to Eutyches.

Among the bishops whose cases were discussed at Chalcedon, two are especially important because of the role their writings will play in the next century. One was Ibas, the bishop of Edessa; the other, Theodoret of Cyrrhus. These two had been condemned along with Flavian at the "Robber Synod." They were now reinstated by the General Council.

At first the Council had no intention of issuing any new formula of faith. It seemed better to settle the problem of Eutyches, and then simply reaffirm the acceptance of the Creed of Nicea and I Constantinople. In the discussions, however, it appeared that the doctrinal points were not entirely clear in the minds of all the bishops; this suggested the need of a further clarifying statement. Moreover, the representatives of the Emperor were most insistent on this in the interests of rooting out once and for all the confusion that had previously reigned.

As a result, in the fifth session (October 22), it was decided to name a special commission to draw up a statement; the papal legates were among those appointed. What they produced is not so much a new Creed as a commentary on the Catholic faith. The first part of the decree is more a statement of what the Church opposes to the teaching of the heresies of the early centuries; the second half is devoted to a more profound explanation of what this doctrine means.

Whatever hesitancies there had been on the part of some bishops because of certain phrases, all questions were satisfactorily answered in the discussions, thanks especially to the explanations of the papal legates. The bishops had all accepted the "Dogmatic Epistle" of Leo earlier, and on October 25, they gathered in solemn session, in the presence of the Emperor and Empress, to sign the dogmatic decree formulated by the Council. The task of the Council, as far as doctrine was concerned, was then finished.

The remaining sessions were concerned mostly with other disciplinary questions. On October 31, thirty canons were issued, of which the twenty-eighth was to be most important. In this canon, the Council of Chalcedon repeated what has been said earlier concerning Constantinople, now the glorious city of the Eastern Empire: "As in all things we follow the ordinances of the holy fathers . . . so do we decree the same in regard to the privileges of the most holy Church of Constantinople, the New Rome. Rightly have the fathers conceded to the see of Old Rome its privileges on account of its character as the imperial city, and moved by the same considerations the 150 bishops [at I Constantinople] have awarded the like privileges to the most holy see of New Rome, judging with good reason that the city which is honored by the imperial power and the senate, and which enjoys the same privileges as the ancient imperial city of Rome, should also be exalted in its ecclesiastical relations and hold the second place after that."

In this way the city of Constantine loomed ever larger on the ecclesiastical horizon. It marks the furthering of the political interests in the East which would contribute eventually to the great break between the Eastern and the Western churches.

The papal legates protested against this canon, but the Council approved. Pope Leo refused to accept the canon, and wrote a series of letters urging the bishop of Constantinople to be content with things as they were. Jerusalem, Alexandria, and Antioch were all more ancient; they were looked upon as apostolic sees, and this canon violated their rights. It should be enough for Constantinople to know it was the imperial city, without wishing to make its civil position determine its ecclesiastical rank.

At the root of this spirit of ambition there was another danger, not mentioned by Leo, that would come to light soon enough in the history of the Church. Rome is the center of Christianity because of the "chair of Peter," and not because of the civil rank of that city. If Leo had accepted the position that the civil importance of a city determines its rank in the Church, the day might come when Rome, having fallen from its lofty civil position, would be challenged as the center of Christianity. This would be contrary to the entire tradition of the Church, which recognized the authority of Peter in Rome, quite independently of the Emperor. Despite Leo's rejection of the canon, however, the spirit remained, and the difficulties which resulted will concern us in later chapters.

The essential work of Chalcedon was accomplished. The faith of the Church of Christ, true God and true Man, was secured once again against the attacks of heresy. What had been achieved in union with Leo was to appear ever more clearly as the work of the Holy Spirit within His Church. What was done apart from Leo, however, would lead only to further dissension and division within the Christian world.

CHAPTER VII . . . *II and III Constantinople*

THE sixth and seventh centuries are marked by new events that prolonged the dispute of Chalcedon. We find here new attempts by the Monophysites to sustain their position; this will bring about two new Councils, and because of their vacillation, will involve two popes — Vigilius and Honorius — in unusual difficulties.

The second Council of Constantinople opened on May 5, 553, in the patriarchal church of that city. In many ways, this was a most surprising Council. For one thing, it was concerned almost entirely with the writings of three men dead for a century and more: Theodore of Mopsuestia (whose teachings had been one of the starting points of Nestorianism); Theodoret of Cyrrhus and Ibas of Edessa (who had been restored to their sees by the Council of Chalcedon). Now 122 years after Ephesus and 102 years after Chalcedon, these three men became the center of attention.

The Monophysites, condemned at Chalcedon, did not die out at once; as with the Arians after Nicea, they continued to promote their own cause. There was much unrest, and a feeling among the Egyptians that Alexandria had come out second best in the debates. This came to the fore especially three years after Chalcedon when Dioscoros, the exiled patriarch of Alexandria, died in exile. In 457, Marcian, the strong defender of Orthodoxy at Chalcedon, also died, and the emperors who followed proved less strong than Marcian. By 475, the Monophysites were once again in power.

Under their influence, a number of decrees appeared which attempted to condemn Chalcedon, or at least ignore it entirely. The two most important were the *Encyclion* of the Emperor Basiliscus and the *Henoticon* of Acacius (the patriarch of Constantinople). Confusion reigned in the East, and it was to Rome that men looked for a solution. Unfortunately there was no longer a Leo sitting on the throne of Peter, and none of the popes of that century succeeded in stamping out the error completely.

In 511, Anastasius, who was over 80 years old, was the emperor; he suddenly decided to impose Monophysitism on the entire empire. Only his death in 518 solved that problem. Under his successor, Justin, the Council of Chalcedon was restored to honor, and men began to speak of a General Council to avoid any further problems. Pope Hormisdas, however, insisted on nothing more than a signing of the formula he had drawn up. Unfortunately, this was to prove insufficient.

Justinian became emperor in 527. This marks one of the great dividing lines in Church history. His wife, Theodora, was to be the cause of further trouble. She was really a Monophysite at heart, and a woman who delighted in interfering with religious matters. Through her influence many of the Monophysites returned, and the problem grew steadily worse. Soon there were Monophysite bishops both at Alexandria and at Constantinople.

About 544 a new attempt was made to discredit Chalcedon. It was a very subtle move, one that hardly mentioned Chalcedon at all. Excerpts from the writings of the three men mentioned above were gathered together, and these writings were now to be condemned. This collection of statements has come to be known as the "Three Chapters." It concerned the writings of Theodore of Mopsuestia, Theodoret of Cyrrhus and Ibas of Edessa.

The Monophysites now pretended that their greatest complaint against Chalcedon was that it had restored Theodoret and Ibas to their sees. It is true that these men had earlier opposed Cyril, and had taught something similar to Nestorianism (the doctrine found in the writings of Theodore of Mopsuestia, and condemned at Ephesus). If the Monophysites now succeeded in condemning these two in particular, and in associating them with the heretic of Mopsuestia, they felt that the Council of Chalcedon would be set in a bad light; it would appear that in restoring Theodoret and Ibas, the Council had approved two heretics.

Justinian favored the condemnation, and most of the Eastern bishops followed his line of thought. Among them were certain other bishops who were not so much Monophysites, but who were now in error because of their revival of the teachings of Origen (who had died in the third century). They were known as the Origenists, and possibly they saw this as an opportunity to distract attention from themselves; the Origenist bishop Askidas was especially active in drawing up the "Three Chapters."

The representative of the Pope at Constantinople, however, refused to sign the condemnation; he perceived clearly the implications. With some reservations concerning the subsequent approval of the Pope, however, Menas, the patriarch of Constantinople, did sign the decree condemning the three men; other bishops followed his lead.

All now looked to Pope Vigilius (537–555) to see what he

would do. Unfortunately, the Pope hesitated. He was forced to come to Constantinople, in 547, where every effort was made to have him sign the condemnation. It had already been realized at Rome and in northern Africa that this could be understood as an attempt to undermine Chalcedon and the teaching of Pope Leo. Vigilius also recognized this, and refused to sign. At a meeting of bishops called to discuss the affair, he broke off negotiations and demanded a written opinion from each bishop.

But then he once again vacillated, and this was his great failing. A stronger man might have avoided a crisis, but Vigilius did not. He issued a *Judicatum* in 548, a decree that condemned the "Three Chapters"; then, in 550, he revoked this statement, deciding with the Emperor to refer the matter to the Council.

His moves were not well received, to say the least. Why he acted as he did is difficult to say: weakness, ambition, fear. The West, however, was greatly upset. One group of African bishops met and attempted to excommunicate the Pope in 550. About the same time, Vigilius decided to excommunicate the leader of the Monophysite group, Askidas, and found himself in trouble in the East; he barely escaped the soldiers of Justinian, and took refuge at Chalcedon in the very same basilica where the now debated decrees had been issued a century before. From here he reorganized his party, and gradually received back some of the excommunicated bishops.

Plans for the Council were under way, however, and Justinian was anxious to go ahead. He realized he had gone too far in his treatment of the aging Pope. Vigilius, however, now disapproved most heartily of the idea of a Council; but he did promise to send on his own statement concerning the problem.

The Council finally opened in 553 at the Church of Sancta Sophia in Constantinople. Hence it is known as II Constantinople. About 150 bishops attended, including 14 from Africa; the

final decree bears 164 signatures. We have only the ancient
Latin version of the Acts; the Greek has been lost.

Eight sessions took place, from May 5 to June 2. The Council
began with the reading of the pertinent decrees and a history
of the dispute. On May 14 the statement of Vigilius arrived,
the *Constitutum*. It was a remarkably well-written theological
work, concerned mostly with the heretical statements of Theodore of Mopsuestia. Vigilius insisted that he would not agree
to a condemnation in any way of Ephesus or Chalcedon, and
for this reason he would not approve of the condemnation of
Theodoret and Ibas. But what was erroneous in Theodore of
Mopsuestia he would agree to condemn.

When the Emperor received this document, he set it aside,
and at once sent other letters and statements to the Council,
containing the former condemnation of the Three Chapters
issued by Vigilius. He ordered the bishops to proceed with the
conciliar decree, and true to fashion they did. On June 2, the
bishops at this Council, not yet approved by the Pope, signed
the final decree. In it they condemned the person and the
writings of Theodore of Mopsuestia, and the writings of Theodoret and Ibas that contradicted St. Cyril's teaching and that
of Ephesus. The errors of these men were summed up in fourteen *anathemata* at the end.

Strangely, though the Council spoke much of Chalcedon, it
was really concerned with Ephesus and Nestorianism. What
was condemned, however, was truly false. There was, nevertheless, a great difference between II Constantinople and Chalcedon. The bishops at Chalcedon had been concerned with the
men, Theodoret and Ibas. When the Council was assured that
they were now once again orthodox in their teaching, they were
restored to their dioceses. II Constantinople, however, was concerned with their *writings*, which were admittedly heretical.
It was most unusual, of course, to begin condemning men a

hundred years after they died, but this is what was done.

Eventually, when Vigilius finally saw that there was now no further danger of seeming to condemn the actions of Chalcedon, he apparently approved the final decree of this Council, as did his successors. It thus became an Ecumenical Council. The secondary purpose of the entire scheme was eventually lost sight of, that is, the attempt to discredit Chalcedon. It was this question of expediency that was the cause of all the hesitancy on the part of Vigilius. His doctrinal position was clear and orthodox; but a stronger man might have taken a definite position from the very start and avoided a great deal of trouble.

At any rate, even under such confused circumstances, the Spirit of Christ triumphed in the Church. Another Christian landmark was sculptured out, and a second resounding condemnation of Nestorianism came forth to guide the Church. Vigilius finally set out for Rome once again, after nine years away, but died on the way. His role was over, but the story did not end there.

One last error was to arise in the seventh century, marking the close of these first disputes about the human nature of Christ. This time the Pope who was to be forever associated with the problem was Honorius (625–638). This also was not simply a doctrinal problem; as might only be expected by this time, politics played a large role in the debates.

In the minds of some, the Council of Chalcedon seemed to have been a triumph of Constantinople over Antioch and Alexandria, the New Rome over the ancient sees. The Egyptians and the Syrians, therefore, both figured prominently in this matter. Wars added to the confusion, as well as new doctrinal disputes among the Monophysites themselves. They all agreed, however, on one point: they wished in some fashion to reject Chalcedon.

The Council of Chalcedon had attempted to break the force

of the Monophysite heresy. By stating clearly that there are in Christ two natures but one Person, the bishops had hoped to accomplish this. But a further question remained, and the teaching about Christ was not finally settled until this had also been debated for a number of decades.

The new error was a combination of many things. The entire question was rephrased. Men no longer asked whether there were "two natures" in Christ. Outwardly, at least, they were anxious to appear loyal to the decree of Chalcedon. They now questioned the "two operations" in Christ — two "activities" in Christ, one human and one divine. Within a rather short time, their question was narrowed down even more, centering on something that really summed up the entire approach: "Did Christ, the Son of God, have one will or two wills?"

This was a very subtle question, and, understood in one sense, it could mean a revival of the Monophysite heresy. If Christ had only *one will*, there would have to be some kind of mixing or confusion of the two wills proper to each nature. The final answer was that Christ had two wills, one divine and one human. If He possessed two complete and perfect natures, Christ would necessarily have had to possess the intellect and the will that belongs to each one of the natures.

When these Monophysites denied that Christ had two wills, they used as their excuse the argument that there could be no "imperfection" of any sort in Christ. Christ was God, and therefore everything must be perfect. Two wills, however, might imply *contrary* wills in Christ, and this would be an imperfection in the God-Man.

There is one sense in which this could be understood correctly. There was no "imperfection" in Christ's human will, since His human will was always in perfect accord with His divine will. They were "one" in that sense; it is what we today would call a "moral union" of the two wills — a union, that is, by way of agreement. But physically there *are* two wills, really distinct from one another; they are "one" only morally, or by reason of their perfect agreement. To hold that Christ had only one physical will would be a rephrasing of the Monophysite error. The will belongs to the nature, and if there is but one will, this can only mean that there is also but one nature.

Thus there were two ways of understanding the phrase "one activity" or "one will." It is not always such a simple thing to understand other people even when we know the meaning of the words they use. Words often imply things far beyond the dictionary meaning. This is what happened in this case.

In the year 610 Sergius became the patriarch of Constantinople; he was to be the strongest defender of this new heresy. Sergius had more than religious views in mind, unfortunately. He was, perhaps foremost, a politician, and a crafty one at that. The Byzantine empire had been divided by the definitions of Chalcedon, and he felt that in his formula he had a means of reuniting the Catholics and Monophysites, politically as well as religiously. The only difficulty was that this meant compromise on doctrinal accuracy, and that means heresy. The viewpoint of Sergius was that if he accomplished his goal of union, the change in formula was really not so great that anyone should be disturbed about it. After all, it was accomplishing a great deal of good, and the entire matter might really be reduced to a dispute over words rather than anything more profound.

Working on this theory, Sergius began to work for Church union. His motto was the phrase "one operation" — one source of action in Christ. He found acceptance among the Monophysites, who were quite ready to admit only one will in Christ, since this followed naturally from their beliefs. Things looked good for reunion; in fact, in 633 a statement of union was signed between Constantinople and Alexandria.

One man, however, saw through the entire question —
Sophronius, a monk at Alexandria. He attempted to point out
the error implied in this formula, but he got nowhere, until,
in his travels, he unexpectedly found himself elected as the
patriarch of Jerusalem!

Sergius could no longer ignore him. Sophronius was too important a man now. The patriarch of Constantinople therefore
wrote an account of the matter to Pope Honorius; the question
was described, however, in terms carefully chosen by the wily
Sergius. His final bit of advice was that all debate on the
matter be forbidden, since further disputes might cause greater
trouble and hinder the work of reunion.

Honorius was not the most brilliant pope to begin with, but
now he was also misinformed. He answered Sergius and unfortunately agreed on the point of allowing no further debate.
This meant that truth was silenced along with error, and that
the error was really free to continue unchallenged. At the same
time, the letter of Honorius indicates that he missed the point
entirely. He answered in terms that discussed the "moral union"
of the two wills in Christ: the human was always in perfect
accord with the divine. The Monophysites, however, were teaching something quite different. They held that there was only
one physical will in Christ, the result of a mixture of the human
and divine. This is why the present heresy is known as "Mo-
nothelitism"; it comes from the Greek word *mono* (one) and
thelema (which means "will"): hence one will.

The "studied obscurity" of Sergius misled the Pope; Honorius
failed to grasp precisely what was going on in the East. What
the Pope had written from Rome was all perfectly true, orthodox
teaching; but it was not the question being debated between
Sergius and Sophronius.

Sophronius continued his defense of the faith, and set forth
the true teaching in clearer fashion, indicating that Christ is

one in regard to His Person (since it is always the same Person who is acting); but that this one divine Person acts in two different natures, either as God (in the divine nature) or as man (in the human nature.)

Honorius did write a second letter that came close to saying the same thing, but he still did not strike out against the precise error of Sergius and his followers. As a result, Sergius continued to gain ground. In autumn of 638, the Emperor Heraclius went even further, and issued a doctrinal decree (the *Ecthesis*) which set forth the doctrine of the Monothelites as the official teaching of the Church; it had been written most likely by Sergius himself.

The problem had now been forced into the light so far that it would eventually have to be solved. Honorius died that same year, and his successors saw the difficulty far more clearly. Pope John IV issued a letter addressed to the Emperor, explaining the true teaching of the two wills, and explaining what Honorius had really been trying to say. But no real progress was made.

Sergius was now dead, as was Pyrrhus, his successor in the see of Constantinople. The new patriarch, Paul, suggested to the Emperor (Constans II) that he issue a new formula to replace the much opposed *Ecthesis*. Thus in 648 there appeared a second imperial decree, the *Typos;* it was still a vague formula, and it added another demand of silence. Error received further help in this regard.

In 649 the new pope, Martin I, made the first decisive move. He held a synod of Western bishops in the Lateran Basilica at Rome. It was not a General Council, but it is justly famous. From this synod there came forth, on the authority of the Pope, a clear-cut statement on the teaching of the Church. It was so clear, in fact, that the opposition to the Catholic party grew vehement; Martin I was rewarded with exile, and died away from Rome in 655. But despite the fact that Monothelite bishops continued to rule in Constantinople, a solution was about to appear. The entire debate began to wither away.

In 668 Constantine IV Pogonatus became the emperor, and he took the initiative in bringing the matter to a final end. In a letter to Pope Donus he suggested a Council; Donus died before the letter reached Rome, in 678. The next pope, Agatho (678–681), agreed to the convocation of the Council. Before sending his representatives on to Constantinople, Agatho summoned a meeting in Rome to formulate the mind of the Western bishops; other gatherings were held elsewhere. These discussions occupied the West until the year 680.

Finally in September of that year, the representatives of the Pope, eleven in all, arrived in the imperial city. The Emperor at once convoked only the bishops pertaining to the patriarch of Constantinople and of Antioch. Apparently it was not at first his intention, nor the intention of the Pope, to summon a General Council; hence the limited call. Bishops from Alexandria and Jerusalem also appeared, so that, from the first session, the Council was really a more universal Council; it was accepted as such by both the Pope and the Emperor. The number of bishops who attended varied somewhat; from 50 at the first session, 174 were present to affix their signature at the signing of the final decree in the eighteenth session. This Council is known as III Constantinople.

The Council opened officially on November 7, 680, in the grand hall of the imperial palace; eighteen sessions were held in all, with the Council ending on September 16, 681. The dogmatic letter of Pope Agatho was read and accepted by all the bishops, who once reflected the acceptance of Pope Leo's letter at Chalcedon: "It is Peter," they cried, "who speaks through Agatho."

The representatives of the Emperor were the honorary presidents of the gathering, but it was the representatives of the

Pope who directed the debate. The entire history of the problem was reviewed; the Monothelites were allowed to state their case. The patriarch of Constantinople received fully the doctrine proposed by Agatho, as did the greater number of bishops present. The patriarch of Antioch, however, held out for his erroneous views and was deposed.

The final decree of the Council served as a summary of the debates concerning Christ during these early centuries. The teaching of Chalcedon was reaffirmed, and to this was added a more precise statement to the effect that those at this Council "likewise proclaim according to the teaching of the holy fathers that Christ has two volitions or wills, and two natural operations without division or change, without partition or co-mingling. And the two natural wills are not opposed (by no means!) as the godless heretics have said; but the human will is compliant, and not opposing or contrary; as a matter of fact it is even obedient to his divine and omnipotent will."

Thus was the question solved. The Council went further in the decree, and censured those earlier men who had been active in promoting this heresy. Strangely, they included the misled Honorius in this list. This was to remain a question for many years: Had the Pope failed the Church? Honorius certainly had failed to grasp the question being debated, but his teaching was accurate enough in what it said. He never intended to "define" any position, as we would view the matter today. His answer was just the opposite: he chose to let matters ride, and avoided even discussing the question.

Agatho had died before the end of the Council, but the next pope, Leo II, approved of its decrees (including the condemnation of Honorius). His approval, in fact, indicates the mind of the Council best of all. Leo explained to the bishops of Spain why Honorius had been condemned: ". . . because instead of extinguishing the incipient flame of heretical doctrine, as befits the holder of apostolic authority, he rather fanned it *by his negligence.*" Had Honorius been less gullible in relying so fully on Sergius, and had he investigated the matter more carefully, much of the trouble could have been avoided. As it was, he unwittingly helped spread the error. But out of this came a fuller understanding of the doctrine concerning Christ, testimony again of the power of God to triumph over the weakness of men within His Church.

WHILE all of these debates were going on in the East concerning the faith of the Church in Christ, other equally important events were taking place in the West. Apart from the Roman pontiffs, a number of Western bishops were involved in the doctrinal debates concerning Christ, but they did not play a dominant role in the entire proceedings. The West was beset by its own difficulties.

In the doctrinal field, there was a long debate that went on in the West that is scarcely mentioned in a history of the Councils: the heresy of the Pelagians and the semi-Pelagians, This was a heresy concerning grace and free will. In a way, it reflected the difference in mentality between the East and the West. The theologians in the East were especially concerned with God Himself, and centered their attention on problems of the Trinity and Christology; those in the West, following the more legal-minded spirit of Rome, developed a special concern for man and his relationship to God's grace.

Pelagius was a British monk who lived in the fifth century. He had spent some time in Rome where he was rather well received as a pious director of souls. After the sack of Rome in the year 410, however, he and his associate, Celestius, came to Carthage, the great see of northern Africa.

At that time, his error came to light and brought forth an immediate reaction on the part of the bishops. Pelagius had overemphasized the power of human nature, and claimed that fallen man could accomplish by his own free will whatever God expected of him. The sin of Adam had harmed him in no way; Adam had affected the rest of mankind only by his bad example. Whatever reward man merited from God, therefore, was in accordance with man's free will. If God gave man any special grace, it would only make it *easier* for man to accomplish the good; he was still capable of doing this, however, without grace.

What this amounted to, of course, was a denial of original sin and of the supernatural order. Man was supreme, and God did nothing more than inspect what man did, and reward him accordingly. Pelagius and his followers were immediately condemned for this teaching; the famous bishop of Hippo, St. Augustine, was their chief opponent. The Catholic Church insisted that man is entirely helpless in the supernatural order, and that, because of Adam's sin, man cannot keep even the requirements of the natural law for any length of time without God's special grace.

In his defense of grace, Augustine naturally stressed the helplessness of man; this brought forth a further reaction. A group of monks near Marseilles concluded that Augustine had not sufficiently safeguarded the *free will* of man; they at once began to attack his position. The Church also condemned their heresy, since in practice it amounted to almost the same teaching as that of Pelagius; hence today we refer to them as the Semi-Pelagians. They insisted that man could, by his own free will, perform at least the "first" act in the supernatural order, the very beginning of faith. After that, they admitted the need of grace; but they felt that to save free will, this first step must come from man. It was seen at once, however, that if, without God's grace, man could perform the *first* act in the way of salvation, it was really man who was saving himself; it was man who started the work of salvation, and what came afterward was secondary and nonessential.

As a result, while the Ecumenical Councils were being held in the East, two especially important local councils were held in the West: the sixteenth Council of Carthage in 418 (which condemned the Pelagians); and the second Council of Orange — in France — in 529 (which condemned the Semi-Pelagians). These were important Councils, not because they were ecumenical in nature, but because of the special approval of two Popes which gave their decrees the importance of dogmatic definitions. Pope Zosimus solemnly approved the decrees of Carthage, and Boniface II approved those of Orange.

These questions of grace were scarcely touched upon by the Ecumenical Councils. The Council of Ephesus briefly reaffirmed the condemnation of the Pelagians in the West. They were important, however, in the history of the times, and of extremely great importance in view of the doctrinal disputes that would arise in later centuries.

In addition to these doctrinal concerns in the West, there was also the problem of the barbarian invasions. The Goths, the Vandals, the Huns, and all such tribes became the special scourge of Europe. The Goths had settled along the shores of the Black Sea and the Danube River, and were perhaps the first to strike. By the beginning of the fourth century, they had already begun to invade their neighbors, and, while some of them had become Christian, they had embraced Arianism in large numbers after Nicea. In this way, the invasions became the means of furthering the error of Arius in Europe.

Some of the tribes passed over into Spain and Italy; others

continued on to northern Africa, bringing new sorrows to the Church during the fifth and sixth centuries. While eventually the Church was to conquer these barbarian hordes by converting them to Catholicism, it would not be accomplished at once. Cities were sacked, monasteries were ruined, and the remains of ancient art and culture were destroyed before their savagery was tamed.

Even the center of Christianity, Rome itself, came under attack. While the Council of Chalcedon was getting under way, guided by the "Dogmatic Epistle" of Leo the Great, this same Pope had to turn his attention to the invasion of the Huns under Attila. Artists have portrayed ever since the picture of the stanch Leo coming forth to meet the invader and preserving Rome, at least temporarily.

About the year 600, Rome knew another Pope who ranks among the great men of history: Gregory the Great (590–604). He does not enter into the history of the Councils, but he is very important in the history of the Church. He came to a Rome that had been crushed by the barbarians and decimated by the plague. He set about reorganizing the papal court. He also concerned himself with the conversion of the barbarians who had brought such destruction; it was the Anglo-Saxons to whom he especially directed his attention. Also, Gregory did much to codify the laws of the Roman Liturgy, establishing the pattern we follow down to this very day.

It is interesting to note in passing another important event during these years. About 570 or 580, Mohammed was born at Mecca in Arabia; by 630 he had returned to capture his home town, and thus became the master of all central Arabia. The event was little noticed by many within the Church, but this far back the stage was set for greater problems in the future; those who embraced the Mohammedan faith were to offer great concern to the popes during the Middle Ages and after.

II Nicea

All of these varied circumstances contributed to bringing about a shift in the center of Christian life: the East now became the pivotal point. Rome as the great imperial city was fast fading. It was now the city of the popes, but it did not as yet have the color of the papal Rome of later centuries. While the triumph of Constantine in 312 had marked one big dividing point in the history of the Church, writers now search for the beginning of a new era. From this point on we face two new cultures: that of Byzantine Christianity in the East, and the start of the Middle Ages in the West. The year 527 — the advent of the Emperor Justinian — has been suggested by some as a convenient peg for the start of this new era; at any rate, the change was surely accomplished by the following century. From this period emerges the history of the Byzantine emperors, who certainly added a new and strikingly different chapter to the story of the Church's life.

With the rise of the Byzantine empire, a new heresy developed; it has come to be known as that of the "Iconoclasts," from the Greek word *eikon* which means "image," and *klaō* meaning "to break." These were the destroyers of images. By the time that Leo III became the Eastern emperor in the year 717, the use of icons or images, both in the West and in the East, had long been a part of Christian life. There are traces of such practices as far back as the first century of the New Testament era. What arose now was the first large attack on the use of images. A similar attack would be repeated in the centuries that lay ahead, but in every instance the answer would be the same: the resounding response of II Nicea, defending the practice and explaining the proper use of images.

For some reason, the emperor, Leo III, developed a conviction that the use of images meant idolatry. It is difficult to single out the precise reason. Leo was, in general, a man who fancied himself a great "reformer" in all fields; this was one aspect of that mentality. The dispute, moreover, was not simply one of a doctrinal nature; it was surrounded by political overtones. The Byzantine emperors all tended to encroach upon the life of the Church. They wished to regulate not only civil matters, but religious questions as well. Thus this controversy was also part of a larger political struggle. This had been true since the days of Constantine himself, and the emperors of the East promoted and opposed heresy at will.

The attitude of Leo may also be a reflection of his earlier religious training. In one instance, he seems to have been associated with a group of Christians who were Manichaeans at heart, and who shared the Manichaean belief that material things were evil in themselves. Thus images would be wrong. His opinions may also be a result of association with the Monophysites. They, too, opposed the veneration of images, since for many of them the "one nature" of Christ was not a true human nature at all, but only some kind of nature that is part human and part divine. Thus an image of Christ would tend to obscure their teaching.

In 726, the Emperor, Leo III, issued the first edict against religious images. This began a long history of opposition to the imperial designs. By this time the practice was properly understood by the people, and it was a part of their Christian way of life. They were not going to cast it aside so easily. It was, of course, not simply a question of having images of Christ and the saints, but also of showing honor or worship of some sort to them. The faithful understood, however, that this was a "relative" honor: in other words, not directed to the images themselves, but ultimately to the person they represent.

In an age when idolatry had not ceased, it is easy to understand how some might confuse this practice with pagan worship. Undoubtedly there were abuses at the time of Leo III as there have been since. The Emperor, however, was not concerned

Council of Ephesus, 431

St. Gregory VII, Pope,
1073–1085

Innocent III, Pope, 1179–1180

Boniface VIII, Pope, 1294–1303

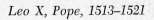
Leo X, Pope, 1513–1521

Paul III, Pope, 1534–1549

Pius IV, Pope, 1559–1565

Council of Trent, 1545–1563

Pius IX, Pope, 1846–1878

*Vatican Council — Pope Pius IX and his Councillors —
1869–1870*

John XXIII, Pope, elected October 28, 1958

with any abuses; it was the practice itself that he attacked, fearing idolatry.

For the idolater, the stone image is the ultimate thing worshiped; this *is* his god. The difference between this and the Christian practice lies in the purpose for the image. Thus in the Old Testament, the same God who said: "Do not make false gods for yourselves," also directed the Jews to fashion the Ark of the Covenant with two cherubim of beaten gold, with "their wings spread out above . . . with their faces looking toward the propitiatory." God had forbidden them to make other "gods" of gold and silver; these images, however, were not their gods.

In the sixteenth century, some of the Reformers revived this dislike of images. They have also come to be known by the same name as their eighth-century counterparts: "Iconoclasts." Zwingli managed to exclude images from the Protestantism of Zurich, on the grounds that they were unscriptural; he rejected organ music in churches for the same reason. Carlstadt adopted the same viewpoint in Germany, with the resulting attacks on statues and crucifixes, smashing them to the floor of the churches. In this, he was opposed by Luther, who was shocked by these proceedings. The Council of Trent was also concerned with the problem, and repeated the answer of II Nicea.

Under Emperor Leo III and his successors a violent desecration of images took place. The icons were broken up; illustrations of Christ and the saints were torn out of manuscripts; relics were cast into the sea. And when the people resisted these imperial moves, prison, exile, torture, and death followed. Much of the brutality and savagery associated with the Byzantine emperors has resulted from their activity in this matter.

Among those sent into exile for refusing to accept the imperial edict on images was Germanus, the patriarch of Constantinople. He was immediately replaced with a more agreeable bishop. With upsets at such a high level, the Pope was naturally involved in the situation, so that the Emperor was soon faced with the authority first of Gregory II, and then of Gregory III. Pope Gregory III (731–741) condemned iconoclasm and, like others before him, Leo made an attempt to kidnap the Pope in Rome and bring him forcibly to Constantinople. The Emperor failed in this, but did manage, by way of getting even, to seize some of the papal land in Sicily and Calabria.

In addition to the Pope, the Emperor was also faced with another great theological opponent, John Damascene. He represents the last of a long line of Greek minds dedicated to the defense of the Catholic faith in these early centuries. Despite his efforts, however, Leo's attitude did not change. Leo's successor, Constantine V, continued the persecution. He took a further step, and convoked a Council of Greek bishops in 753 at the imperial palace at Hieria. This ranks with the other pseudo-councils of history, since the Pope was not invited; nor, for that matter, were the other Oriental patriarchs. Nevertheless, over 300 bishops met and signed the imperial decree which condemned the use and the honoring of sacred images.

This Council brought a fresh impetus to the struggle between the opposing parties. The dispute was to be solved only through a General Council, held eventually at Nicea. Constantine V died in 775, thus opening the way for a settlement. His son, Leo IV, ruled only five years, and while he did not stop the movement, he did slow down the progress. When he died in 780, his wife, the Empress Irene, took over the government as the regent for her young son, Constantine VI. Irene was most favorable to the traditional Catholic faith, and at once set about restoring the ancient practices.

This chain of circumstances presents us with one of the unusual elements of II Nicea. What theologians today will call the "material convocation" was accomplished by a woman, the

Empress Irene! She also presided at the final solemn session, and, as Eastern empress, signed the official document.

In December of 784, Irene named Tarasius as the new patriarch of Constantinople. Tarasius belonged to the group that favored the use of images, and on the very day of his election demanded publicly that Irene convoke a General Council to restore unity to the Church.

Pope Adrian I (772–795) was invited to attend the Council, and he agreed; he would send his legates to represent him. He set forth certain conditions, however, under which he would participate. Above all the Empress was to guarantee the freedom of the Council. In addition, the pseudo-council of Hieria must be condemned. These conditions were accepted and fulfilled. The Council was set for August, 786, at Constantinople.

The gathering got off to a bad start, however. The army turned against the Empress, and an uprising of the Iconoclasts got out of hand. The Council dissolved at once, and the papal legates set out for Rome. Irene purged the army of disloyal subjects, and thus assured that there would be no recurrence, the Council met a second time on September 24, 787. This time the meeting was held at Nicea, the city in which the very first General Council had taken place. Thus it became II Nicea.

About 300 bishops gathered in the Church of St. Sophia, including the papal legates and the representatives of the Empress. In addition, a large number of monks and clerics were also present. Tarasius, the patriarch of Constantinople, presided. The dominant role, however, was played by Pope Adrian I. Just as the "Dogmatic Epistle" of Pope Leo the Great dominated the scene when it was read at the Council of Chalcedon, so here did the Epistle of Pope Adrian set the tone of the gathering. At the first session his letter explaining the traditional faith of the Church was read aloud, and the bishops voted to accept the teaching of Adrian. For practical purposes, the doctrinal question was settled from that moment on.

There were in all eight sessions between September 24 and October 23, 787. The pseudo-council of Hieria was condemned; scriptural texts and statements from the Fathers were brought forth in evidence of the traditional practice; and finally a dogmatic decree was formulated stating precisely the Catholic teaching. All the bishops signed after the papal legates, as well as a number of the Iconoclast bishops who had been received back after a profession of faith.

The final session was held in Constantinople at the Magnaura Palace. The Empress presided, and her young son, Constantine, was also present. They both signed the official decree after it had been read. The Empress thus approved the decisions of the Council. Now only the Pope's acceptance was needed. Adrian approved of the solemn decree. But he did not send a letter to the Empress, as was usually the custom, since there was another matter that had not been solved at the Council. Adrian was conscious of that fact, and he had directed his legates to attend to it. The earlier emperors had taken over some of the papal lands, and, even more important, by doing this they had encroached upon the papal rights. Adrian had already experienced the problems associated with the Byzantine emperors. He did not want to give the impression, by a formal letter of approval, that he agreed with this challenge to the spiritual power of the popes, which underlay the imperial action. He did, however, approve of the doctrinal decree, and thus II Nicea ranks as an Ecumenical Council.

The honor given to images was settled once and for all. The Council was careful to add that it is quite proper to light vigil lights before statues of Christ and the saints, or to burn incense before them, and it explained the reason why:

"We define with all certainty and diligence that as the figure of the precious and life-giving Cross, so also the venerable and holy images, both painted and of stone and of other proper material, should be set up in the holy churches of God. . . . The more frequently they are seen by a pictorial representation, the more readily those who contemplate the images are aroused to a remembrance and desire of those they represent . . . and are aroused to bestow upon them a respectful devotion — not, however, true adoration (*latria*), which, according to our faith and as is becoming, is bestowed upon the divine nature alone."

Centuries later the Council of Trent would give the same answer to the Iconoclasts of the sixteenth century, recalling the words of II Nicea:

"The images of Christ, of the Virgin Mother of God, and of other saints are to be kept with honor in places of worship especially; and to them due honor and veneration is to be paid — not because it is believed that there is any divinity or power intrinsic to them for which they are reverenced, nor because it is from them that something is sought, nor that a blind trust is to be attached to images as it once was by the Gentiles who placed their hope in idols; but because the honor which is shown to them is referred to the proto-types which they represent."

After II Nicea, the heresy of the Iconoclasts lay dormant for the time. It was to arise again in 813 under Emperor Leo V. But in 842 another woman ruled in place of her infant son, this time Theodora. With the help of St. Methodius, who replaced the Iconoclast patriarch of Constantinople, she was able to give the decrees of II Nicea once again the respect due them as a Council of the Holy Spirit.

It seemed that finally peace would reign in the East. Almost continually since the time of Constantine there had been doctrinal problems tearing asunder that part of the Church; time and again there had been conflict between the emperors and the popes; the bishops had rejected the Supreme Pontiff and cast their lot with the king. All of this turmoil, however, was now about to boil over, worse than ever before. What had been brewing underneath, throughout all these other disputes, was a rejection of papal authority. This was now to come to the fore and eventually lead to a split in Christianity that has not been repaired to this day.

CHAPTER IX ... *IV Constantinople*

THE controversy with the Iconoclasts began to have a more far-reaching effect both in Rome and in Constantinople. The Eastern bishops had once again been cut off from Rome, both because of the persecution and because of their acceptance of heresy. This had only deepened the tendency to act independently of the Bishop of Rome. The popes, on the other hand, became increasingly distrustful of the East, and of the Eastern emperors especially. These rulers had often fostered heresy; some of them now played a major role in promoting a new error, and had at the same time begun to encroach upon the rights of the papacy.

As a result, the Roman pontiffs began to look elsewhere for support, and this time they chose a ruler of the West. The Byzantine kingdom would continue at least until the fall of Constantinople in 1453, but the close relationship with the papacy ceased after II Nicea. The new papal liberator was to be Charlemagne, and the year 800, when he was crowned Roman Emperor by Pope Leo III, marks a further dividing point in the history of the Church.

About the time of II Nicea and the Iconoclast heresy in the

East, a struggle for power was continuing in the West between the Franks and the Lombards. In 768 Charlemagne had succeeded his father, Pepin, as leader of the Franks. By 773 he had invaded the Lombard kingdom and was prepared to secure Italy for himself. By the time Pope Leo III was elected in 795, Charlemagne was well on his way toward being an important man in Rome. Moreover, when the Pope ran into difficulties in Rome, he turned to the King of the Franks for assistance. This led, almost by necessity, to the final step: on Christmas day of the year 800, Charlemagne knelt before Pope Leo III in St. Peter's at Rome and was crowned Holy Roman Emperor.

While the papacy was cementing its ties more closely with the West, another situation was developing in the East which would lead to a final and lasting break with Rome. In 842 the Empress Theodora had come to power and had managed to overcome the last traces of the Iconoclast heresy. Methodius, the patriarch of Constantinople who had aided her in this move, died in 846; he was succeeded by Ignatius, a devout man in his own way, but one who seemed to make enemies easily. Theodora had now retired, and it was Bardas, her brother, who acted as regent for the young Emperor Michael III.

Bardas was far from a saintly man, and when he continued his scandalous way of life, Ignatius finally refused to permit him to receive Communion on the feast of the Epiphany, 857. Bardas was infuriated, and finally managed to banish Ignatius. The see of Constantinople was taken over by Photius in 858.

It is not easy to determine what sort of man Photius was. He may not have been the unscrupulous plotter some would have him; on the other hand, his wily ways could not all have been the result of pure chance. He was a layman, but apparently a devout person and a truly learned individual. Nevertheless his election was pushed through in no time at all, and contrary to the demands of Church law. For one thing, there had been force used in removing the former bishop; the prelate who consecrated Photius was under a cloud at Rome; and finally the entire move from layman to patriarch was accomplished in only six days.

In the following year, Photius sent a letter to Pope Nicholas I, asking for his approval, and remarking how this heavy burden had really been thrust upon him against his will. Rome, however, was perhaps universally suspicious of moves in the East by this time; experience had taught them to be cautious. As a result, before approving Photius, Nicholas decided to send two representatives to Constantinople to investigate. They were empowered to approve the new patriarch if all went well.

For whatever reasons given them, the two legates agreed to the deposition of Ignatius and the approval of Photius. In a gathering of over 300 bishops at Constantinople in the year 861, they signed the proper papers. It appeared later, however, that a large number of witnesses had been "bought" to testify against Ignatius at this meeting; this may well explain the error.

By this time, the friends of the ousted patriarch, Ignatius, who had been kept from reaching Rome, finally got to the Pope and told them his half of the story. The Pope thereupon refused to recognize the acts of this meeting of 861, or to ratify the decisions of his legates. In 863 he called a synod at Rome in which Photius was declared as stripped of all ecclesiastical dignity.

This made little difference to Photius. He supported his position by the actions of the papal legates, and even went a step further: he set out to attack the Pope directly. Photius decided to summon a council of his own which would depose Pope Nicholas I. He contacted the other Eastern patriarchs, writing a letter that violently accused the Western Church of heresy. As in all of the debates to follow, so now the attention was centered especially on disciplinary and liturgical matters. It was claimed that the Western Church looked down on married priests; it made use of unleavened bread; it advised fasting on Saturdays, and the like.

Among them was an accusation of heretical teaching that was to play a larger role in later Councils. The West had added the *"Filioque"* to the Creed: a Latin phrase meaning "and the Son." It was used to explain the relationship of the Holy Spirit to the other divine Persons. Thus the West now prayed: "We believe in the Holy Spirit . . . who proceeds from the Father *and the Son.*" This phrase will concern us later on. It was Photius, however, who especially considered this heretical.

The other bishops failed to co-operate much in the Council of Photius. In the summer of 867 this meeting was held, and a decree deposing the Pope was signed by twenty-one others. Photius managed to forge another thousand names, however, and the document seemed quite formidable.

The scene then changed rapidly. In September of that same year, the history of assassinations that tends to make Byzantine history so colorful added the names of Bardas and his nephew, Michael III. The victor was Basil, who was now proclaimed emperor; he promptly took steps to get rid of the former favorites, including Photius.

Basil was especially interested in reuniting the clerics of his kingdom. They had now been separated into two groups for ten years: the Ignatians and the Photians. The Emperor immediately recalled Ignatius and cast out Photius; he then asked the Pope for a General Council. By the time his letters reached Rome, Nicholas I was dead and a new pope, Adrian II, received them. Adrian agreed to the Council, and as a preliminary held a synod at Rome in June, 869, in which Photius was condemned and the decrees of Ignatius confirmed. Basil accordingly convoked the Council to be held that year at Constantinople, known now as IV Constantinople.

IV Constantinople

The eighth General Council got under way on October 5, 869. The papal legates arrived in September with orders to receive signatures on the decree of the Roman synod, and to reinstate Ignatius. They could also receive back the schismatics who agreed to sign, but Photius himself was to be punished.

At the opening session there were only twelve bishops admitted to the Church of St. Sophia. In addition to these, there were the three papal legates, two delegates from the patriarchs of Jerusalem and Antioch, and Ignatius himself — a total of eighteen, plus the representatives of the Emperor. There were reasons for this, of course. After ten years, the number of bishops appointed by Ignatius had decreased, and the number of Photian bishops increased proportionately; but the Photian bishops had been automatically excluded. Among the others, there was the prerequisite of signing the decree of the Roman synod before entering the conclave, and some hesitated to do this. It is possibly indicative of the general spirit, however, that in 861 Photius had gathered together over 300 bishops to depose Ignatius, and now, eight years later, only 102 attended the papal conclave, and this at the final session.

There were eight sessions held between October 1 and November 5. The number of bishops grew each day as more and more signed. At the fifth session Photius himself was present, but refused to discuss the matter; when he did speak, it was generally in imitation of Scripture, adapting, for example, the words of Christ: "My justification is not of this world."

By request of the Emperor, who attended the sixth session, the Photian bishops were eventually allowed to enter. They heard the decrees and were given seven days to decide on their position. There was a three-month interval between the eighth session and the last two, which were held on February 12 and 28, 870. This was possibly done to allow time for some of the more distant bishops to arrive.

When the Council came to an end, the teaching of Photius had been condemned, and his writings burned; many of the bishops had been received back to union with the Pope; the false witnesses of the illegal council of Photius had been dealt with; and Photius himself had been sent into exile. At the final session, held in the presence of the Emperor, twenty-seven canons were issued, as well as a lengthy dogmatic decree. The work of IV Constantinople was over officially, but — as might be expected — the matter did not end there.

The papal legates finally managed to get back to Rome in December of 870, having fallen into the hands of pirates on the way. Pope Adrian II officially confirmed the Council in 871. But by 877 the characters in this drama had exchanged parts once again. Ignatius had apparently fallen into disfavor with the next pope, John VIII; this may possibly have been due to difficulties with the Bulgarian king. In the meantime, Photius had returned to favor with Basil, the emperor, and by 873 was back in the imperial palace. When Ignatius died in 877, Photius, strange to say, returned once again to the throne as patriarch of Constantinople!

It was not known in Rome that Ignatius had died, and John VIII had determined to take more harsh steps against him. Thus he threatened Ignatius that if he did not manage to settle affairs between the Greeks and the Bulgarians, he himself would be deposed; in April, 878, he sent his legates to Constantinople with this message.

The legates were quite astounded to find Photius as the patriarch; they had come to deal with Ignatius! They attempted to act in a most diplomatic manner, and neither condemned nor approved Photius; they referred the matter to John VIII. The Pope decided to recognize Photius, provided the patriarch publicly signified his change of attitude. This was accomplished at a synod at Constantinople in 879, where the difficult matters were at least sufficiently well mended to preserve peace for a time. Photius again fell into disfavor with the next emperor, Leo VI; thus he passes out of history in 886 when Leo became the ruler.

The entire history of Photius was but an episode; the actual separation between Constantinople and Rome was relatively short. But the case had extremely grave consequences. For one thing, it brought into the open the antagonisms against Rome that had been lurking beneath the surface of the Eastern mind. Even more to the point, however, it marked a change in attitudes. While earlier patriarchs and bishops had been concerned about defending the East against the "pretensions" of Rome, Photius had now directly attacked the papacy and accused the West of heresy.

Thus it was the "spirit" of Photius that was to dominate the Eastern Church in later centuries. While at the time of the break in the eleventh century, his name was scarcely mentioned, the seed of discord that he had sown came to full growth. As we may note later, in the discussions concerning the procession of the Holy Spirit at II Lyons and Florence, it was to Photius that the Greek theologians turned for support. His name became the rallying cry for those opposed to reunion.

The history of IV Constantinople and the later approval of Photius by John VIII indicate the vagaries of the time, and the tensions that abounded between the East and the West in the ninth century. This state of affairs continued throughout the next century, and led directly to the final break in the century following, the eleventh.

By the time that Michael Cerularius became the patriarch of Constantinople in 1043, there was practically no contact at all between Rome and the East. The situation has been best described as that intermediate stage between peace and war, marked by a break in diplomatic relations. It was to be Cerularius who would take the decisive step that would upset the balance and force open warfare.

Michael Cerularius tended to look upon himself as a most important man, and, to be truthful, he was. He easily stands out among the other personages of that period in the East. He had earlier had contact with the imperial court, but had entered a monastery from which his old friend, Constantine IX, summoned him when he became emperor.

About 1053, steps were taken to mend the political fences between the East and the West. Troubled by the invasion of the Normans, Pope Leo IX and the Western emperor, Henry III, were ready to form an alliance with Constantine IX. This was not particularly pleasing to Michael Cerularius, however. He fully realized that such political union among the princes would eventually mean giving up the religious independence that he enjoyed as patriarch of Constantinople. Cerularius, if he was anything, was ambitious. He dealt with the Emperor more as an equal power, collaborating in the achievement of a common goal. He rather entertained the hope of playing the same role in the East that the Pope enjoyed in the West.

Reading the signs of the time, Cerularius adopted the old principle that offense is the best defense. In order to preserve his power, it was necessary to attack. What appeared, then, was a famous letter, presumably written by Leo, the bishop of Achrida in Bulgaria. It was addressed to John, the bishop of Trani in Italy; but it was easily enough seen that Cerularius was behind the letter.

The bishop of Trani was a Latin, but the diocese was in Byzantine Italy; as such, he was a subject of the Byzantine Emperor. The letter speaks of the question of union between Rome and Constantinople; and it more or less takes for granted that there had been a break. It is careful to point out, however, that there are obstacles involved. The West has fallen into heresy — naming again the familiar themes already brought forth by Photius: the use of unleavened bread, the addition of the *"Filioque,"* and so forth.

The letter ends with an exhortation to the bishop of Trani to correct his errors, noting that Christ wishes not the death of the sinner, but that he repent and live. The tone of condescension was apparent; it reflected the spirit of a superior speaking to a wayward subject. The letter was written in order to discuss the problem of reunion, but the tone made more than evident that just the opposite was desired. For a diplomatic note, it could not have been more tactless, and Cerularius was not the man to bungle in such a manner.

What was said, of course, was not intended just for the bishop of Trani. It was written especially for the eyes of Rome, and the letter soon arrived there. Cerularius knew the reaction that might be expected at Rome, and his expectations were fulfilled. In this way, he had managed to promote a definite break, but he had attempted to maneuver Rome into a position in which it would appear that *Rome* had caused the break. This diplomatic technique is recognized better today than in the eleventh century, despite all the intrigue of that period.

Correspondence between Rome and Constantinople followed quite naturally. The answer of Pope Leo IX was drafted by his chief adviser, Cardinal Humbert. Humbert was a true reformer, a very learned man, but absolutely no diplomat. He was content to state the truth bluntly, even dramatically, and ignore the obvious reactions. The Church, however, is a group of human beings, and even in stating the truth, this fact must be taken into consideration. There are more as well as less diplomatic ways of stating the same thing with equal force. Humbert usually managed to choose the less diplomatic means.

The turn in political and military fortunes of the Pope seemed to indicate to Constantine IX that reunion was advisable. The

Normans had already imprisoned the Pope at Benevento, and there he received rather conciliatory letters from Constantinople. It was decided, therefore, to send on a papal legation, headed by Cardinal Humbert; the representatives were empowered to settle the case.

Again Humbert wrote two letters for the Pope, one to the Emperor and the other to Michael Cerularius, with the same lack of diplomatic skill. On the eve of a mission of reconciliation, these letters bitterly attacked the patriarch of Constantinople and his ambitious manners; they also undertook to defend the Western practices criticized by the East. Cerularius was simply told what he had to do, in the bluntest possible fashion. This was his duty to Rome. Should he refuse, he would be justly relegated to the realm of the heretics and the synagogue of Satan.

The tone of these letters alone would have doomed the mission, but Cerularius became even more incensed at the preliminary visit of the papal legates to Argyros, the chief Byzantine official in Italy. Cerularius was most hostile to Argyros, and had even excommunicated him. Hence he used this visit as an occasion to deny that the papal legates were the authentic representatives of the Pope. They were only the tools of Argyros.

The legates had determined to deal with the Emperor first, and when they arrived at Constantinople in the spring of 1054 they ignored Cerularius and he ignored them. Matters grew worse in April, when Pope Leo IX died; his successor was not elected until September, and did not take possession of the see of Rome until April of 1055. Thus Humbert and his two companions were on their own.

Not being able to negotiate with Cerularius, Humbert engaged in a learned dispute with a monk, Nicholas Stethatos, at the monastery of Studios. As usual, the debate was marked by the violent terms of the Cardinal. In June, a final dispute was held before the Emperor, and Nicholas submitted; his books were burned and he was reconciled to Rome.

During all these months, Cerularius continued to ignore the legates, consistently refusing to meet with them, despite the Emperor's pleas. The legates came to the conclusion that not even the Emperor could persuade the patriarch to change, so they decided to leave Constantinople. Before they left, however, Humbert had one more card to play. He wished to take his leave with a resounding crash, and he did.

On July 16, 1054, the papal legates went to the Church of St. Sophia at the hour of the solemn liturgy. They entered the building and publicly protested against the obstinacy of the patriarch. Then, in view of the clergy and people, they went to the principal altar and carefully laid upon it the bull of excommunication they had prepared. The bull included Cerularius and all who followed him. They then walked out of the great church, and left Constantinople two days later.

There was an attempt to recall them from the port, and they did return to Constantinople. They left again at once, however, perhaps with good reason. The city was incensed. Cerularius had made public the bull of excommunication, and once again Humbert had given vent to his sharp pen. He did state the dogmatic truths concerning the primacy of the Roman see, but he then went on in most virulent fashion to attribute practically every heresy of history to the Eastern Church.

The Emperor appeased the city by having the bull of excommunication burned. In July of that year a synod was called to condemn the acts of the Roman legates. In later discussions, not only Cardinal Humbert was attacked, but also the entire Western Church. The position of Cerularius was adopted universally. The Eastern Church had separated from Rome.

Some of the patriarchs of the other cities tried in vain to appease the wrath of Cerularius, but to no avail. By 1058,

Michael Cerularius was dead, but he lived on as a symbol of the breach that continues to this day. The break had been developing for centuries; it might only have been expected. The patriarch of Constantinople, in 1054, however, took the decisive step, and because of this he became the hero of the East, and a patron saint of the Byzantine Church.

IV Constantinople had striven valiantly to defeat the process of separation, but God still permits human weakness to run its course. Nevertheless the Council did draw up the pattern of what can be accomplished. The solution to the briefer schism of Photius may yet point the way toward mending the break caused by Cerularius, which has already existed over 900 years too long.

CHAPTER X . . . *I–IV Lateran*

THE Middle Ages have become increasingly important in the eyes of more recent historians. There had been a time when some men tended to almost write them out of history, for they were supposedly centuries of ignorance and superstition, and nothing more. We have come to realize, however, the close relationship they bear to an understanding of the culture and civilization of the Western world today.

We might divide the entire period into three sections. The early period began at least with the time of Charlemagne (800) if not before; the high point was reached in the thirteenth century; and a period of decline set in from the end of that century until the fall of Constantinople and the rise of Humanism and the Renaissance in the fifteenth century.

During these ages we meet the first General Councils held in the West, and the first Councils convoked both formally and materially by the Roman pontiffs themselves. The story of the Church during these years is very much a tale of the struggle on the part of the spiritual to overcome the worldly. The Church had to free itself from the interference of the temporal rulers, both in the East and the West; it had to fight for the rights which belonged to it as a spiritual organization, the Body of Christ Himself.

On the other hand, this same Church had to struggle against the sinfulness of its own members. The Church is a group of people, joined to Christ in the work of saving mankind. But those people, no less than those not yet joined to this Body of Christ, bear the weakness of Adam. Fallen nature is not destroyed by grace, but perfected. There always remains, therefore, the danger of man's rejection of grace, and the reappearance of his all too weak humanity.

When we consider the Councils of the Middle Ages, then, we must look frequently at these two problems: the struggle against temporal rulers who would draw the Church away from its spiritual purpose, and the effort to overcome the sinfulness of her weak members, both high and low. Thus the first Councils of the Middle Ages, and the first of the West, were largely Councils of reform — reform aimed at a very high level, that of the bishops and the clergy. They were held in Rome at the mother church of Christianity, the Pope's own church as bishop of Rome, St. John Lateran. Hence they are known as the Lateran Councils.

There has always been a danger in the Church of having men attach themselves to individuals *within* the Church rather than to the Church itself. Even today there are cases of people who join the Church because of the striking personality of one priest, and of others who leave it because of the harshness or sinfulness of another. Neither of these are valid reasons for joining or leaving the Church, for one is to believe in Christ. Nothing that any Catholic — priest or laymen, bishop or even pope — may do can destroy the Church which Christ established. It seems that God wanted to emphasize this in the evils He permitted within His Church; they were singled out for special notice during these centuries.

The history of the Councils of the Middle Ages is much of a confirmation of this truth. Had the Church of Christ rested upon the strength of men alone, their human weakness would long ago have sent it toppling to the ground. From a purely human standpoint, there was nothing that could have happened to ruin the Church that did not actually take place. Yet the Church survived because it is sustained not by men but by God.

It is important to realize this in order to understand the problems of the Middle Ages. This was not the only time, of course, when this lesson was taught. Earlier, in the third century, the followers of Cyprian had been led into error by holding that a man who did not have faith could not baptize validly. This really implied that the faith came from the man and not from God; but the Church teaches that the man is simply the instrument. The same thing would be implied at the time of the Protestant Revolt, when it was held that a priest in the state of mortal sin could not administer a life-giving sacrament, implying again that the grace came from the instrument himself instead of from God. It was not actually an overspiritualized approach to the Church that led the Protestants of the sixteenth century into error. It came, rather, from a too human notion of that Church. They tended to identify the spiritual powers of the Church too closely with the weakness of the men who act as God's instruments. As a result, they even went further than they themselves had intended at first, and instead of purifying the human instruments, they ended up by rejecting the visible nature of Christ's Church on earth.

There were four General Councils held at the Lateran in rather quick succession — four in about 90 years: 1123, 1139, 1179, 1215. They were all remarkably similar in character, and were concerned primarily with Church reform. The first three were held during the Lenten season; the fourth in November. They accomplished their tasks with a small number of public sessions, with private meetings taking place in between. They also reflect a typical difference between the Eastern and the Western mind. The earlier Councils in the East were primarily concerned with dogmatic problems, the doctrine of faith; they discussed disciplinary problems, but as a more secondary concern. The four Lateran Councils, however, dealt primarily with canonical and juridical questions; doctrinal problems play a secondary role in the over-all picture. This difference in approach was brought on, of course, by the nature of the problems they faced, but it is also indicative of the Roman mind which tends naturally to a more legal point of view.

The Lateran Basilica had been the scene of ten or more local or Western synods that we know of. In 1122, Pope Callixtus II announced by way of a letter to the bishops and princes of the Christian world that he now intended to convoke a "General Council" at the Lateran in 1123. This Council was to be concerned with the great and diverse problems which faced the Church at that time.

In point of fact, the most noteworthy act of the Council was the reaffirmation of what is known as the "Concordat of Worms." Especially after the time of Charlemagne, there had developed a notion of the "bishop" that included two elements: he was both a religious pastor and a feudal lord. From this notion there arose the question as to whether the Pope or the Emperor had the right to confer on the bishop his authority in the temporal order. What made the problem especially difficult was the general conviction that the office of bishop was a unified thing; the bishop was simultaneously priest and temporal ruler.

The emperors argued that just as they confer all civil honors and benefices within their realm, so also they had the right to confer this civil honor on the bishop. But in practice it was difficult to see how the Emperor was not also bestowing the spiritual power; this was emphasized all the more by the fact that the Emperor or prince adopted the practice of giving the ring and the crosier. What was implied was that once the ruler had made his choice, the faithful were expected to applaud the move and the clergy were to proceed with the consecration. This easily led to serious confusion and to obvious abuses. If the Emperor had such absolute power, he was able to name almost anyone — fit or unfit — for the office of bishop, and others would have to go along with his decisions.

Already in the eleventh century, Pope Gregory VII (Hildebrand) had fought for the spiritual independence of the Church in this regard; the popes who followed him continued the battle. Things finally came to a head in the dispute between Callixtus II and the emperor, Henry V. At a meeting held at Worms in September of 1122, a clear distinction was drawn between the spiritual power of a bishop and his temporal power. The spiritual power came from the Church only; the temporal ruler granted only the rights to the temporal rule now associated with the office.

Henry V accepted this position, and a compromise was made. The agreement most probably represented only a temporary provision insofar as Germany was concerned; what the Church had been striving for was granted fully in the territories outside of Germany. Thus, in Germany itself, the Emperor was to preside over the election of a new bishop, guaranteeing its complete freedom. He was then permitted to bestow the temporal power on the one so chosen by means of the scepter; he promised to give up forever the bestowal of the ring and crosier, the special signs of spiritual power. After this ceremony, the clergy would proceed to the consecration of the new bishop (or abbot).

Outside of Germany, however, the Emperor had no part at all in the elections; he could, moreover, bestow the temporal power by means of the scepter only after the Church had performed the sacred rights of consecration. This was the ideal, of course, and it is what we are generally accustomed to thinking of today in regard to the election of bishops. Thus *lay investiture,* as this practice was called, came to an end.

What the I Lateran Council did above all was to confirm the Concordat of Worms. About 300 or more bishops, perhaps as many as 500, as well as many abbots, gathered at the Lateran Basilica on the Third Sunday of Lent in 1123 and set about this task. We have no records of what took place; we have only the canons issued by them. Two or three other sessions apparently took place after the opening session on March 18; the Council seems to have been finished by the end of March. There were also some twenty-two canons issued in regard to Church reform, similar to those repeated in the next Council.

In April of 1139, the II Council of the Lateran took place under Pope Innocent II. Again we know very little of the history of this gathering or of its proceedings; it seems that no one who took part in the Council left any record of it. The canons issued by the Council, however, give us an indication of the general problems it faced.

In all of these Councils there was a recurring problem of schism within the Western Church; it was only a faint hint at the great schism yet to come. In 1118, before the Emperor Henry V had signed the Concordat at Worms, he had attempted to set up an antipope, Gregory VIII (just as his predecessor, Henry IV, had tried to introduce the antipope, Clement III). Later on, when Pope Innocent II had been elected in 1130, a new dispute arose over his election; a number of other cardinals proceeded to elect the antipope, Anacletus II. This question, then, had to be treated at II Lateran, in 1139.

Pope Innocent II summoned a General Council to consider the general needs of the Church — the question of the antipope especially, but also the matter of reform, and the condemnation of heretical teachings. The Council was held in April of 1139. Possibly 500 or 600 bishops and abbots attended, along with many others; a total of about 1000.

The antipope had already died in 1138; at this point his acts were declared to be void. In addition, those who had rallied about him were also punished; Innocent II was especially severe in this regard. The center of attention then passed on to the need for reform, particularly among the clergy. This entire period is marked by failings that were rooted out only with the greatest difficulty. As long as lay investiture continued, many men became bishops with the temporal power only in mind; they had no concern for the spiritual. They engaged in simony — the buying and selling of spiritual favors; they had no training for their priestly work; they disregarded clerical celibacy entirely. St. Bernard (who died in 1153) set out to preach against these manifold abuses in his time, and the Lateran Councils all set down laws intended to eradicate them.

Although the II Lateran Council was a great triumph for Innocent II, it failed to achieve all of the goals intended; it was one thing to make laws and quite another to enforce them among unwilling subjects. The Council was not greatly concerned with doctrinal questions, but it did denounce the teaching of Peter of Bruys who was preaching a form of Manichaeanism (the basic tenet being that material things are evil in themselves). In the back of this there was the foreshadowing of the antisacrament and antipriest spirit that would come to full growth at the time of the Reformation. This was also detected in the condemnation of Arnold of Brescia. Although he would later become more extreme, still at this time he so emphasized the fact that the Church ought to possess no property that he invited the further conclusion that the Church is "not of this world" in any sense, and thus is really an "invisible body."

The III Lateran Council took place in March of 1179 under Pope Alexander III. This Pope had also been engaged in conflict with a temporal ruler — Frederick Barbarossa. This rather changeable character had been crowned emperor in 1155 by Pope Adrian IV, the only Englishman to have been pope. By 1158, however, he was involved in a dispute over the relationship of the Christian Emperor to the Pope, a dispute that reached a crisis with the death of Adrian in 1159. At that time, a schism threatened the Church, and two men were again contesting for the papal throne: Alexander III, and a man more favorable to Frederick, who called himself Victor IV.

Frederick attempted to solve this dispute by summoning a Council, after the manner of the Eastern emperors. Alexander III, however, refused to consent to such a Council. Nevertheless a small gathering was held at Pavia, and the antipope, Victor, was accepted officially by the Emperor. Nevertheless, the true pope, Alexander III, continued to gather more supporters; he eventually excommunicated the Emperor for his role in the pseudo-council. Frederick attacked Italy, however, and the Pope had to flee Rome.

The triumph of the Emperor continued until 1176 when finally the opposing forces conquered him at the battle of Legnano; in the following year he recognized Alexander as pope, kneeling before him to beg absolution. For the first time since he was elected pope — eighteen long years — Alexander III (one of the greatest personages of the Middle Ages) was free to settle down in Rome and attend to the works of the Church.

Alexander's first thought was a General Council to correct the evils that this bitter division had wrought. Thus in March of 1179 the III Lateran Council met to restore the discipline of the Church. We know little of its history. Somewhere between 300 and 600 bishops and abbots attended; there were three public sessions.

Once again, the acts of the antipopes were annulled; there had been three in all — two successors of Victor IV. Those who took part in the schism were reconciled after they recited an oath of loyalty to the legitimate Pope. In order to avoid a recurrence in the future, the regulations in regard to the papal election were made more precise, demanding a two-thirds majority of the votes; no mention was made of any approval by the Emperor nor of any role to be played by the people or the other members of the clergy.

The special concern of this Council, as with the other Lateran Councils, was the matter of reform. Some twenty-seven canons were issued, similar to those of the earlier gatherings, but more detailed. There had been an attempt to contact the Greek schismatics, but they reached no agreement at the Council. One of the canons spoke of the new heresies that had begun to crop up in parts of Europe — that of the Waldensians and that of the Albigensians. The IV Lateran Council, however, would have to deal with these in greater detail.

None of the earlier Councils had achieved the sweeping reforms that were needed and that many had desired, so that in 1213 Pope Innocent III (1198–1216) announced his intention of calling a fourth General Council at the Lateran. He sent out letters to all the bishops, princes, and heads of religious orders, setting the Council for November, 1215. He was most insistent that all attend, and pointed out in advance that an excuse such as the difficulty of travel would not be valid. Innocent succeeded. The IV Lateran Council was the greatest of the four — the crowning point of the thirteenth century (which, in turn, was the crowning point of the entire Middle Ages). To the people of Rome, it seemed as if the whole world had shown up. Over 400 bishops were there, including the patriarchs of Jerusalem and of Constantinople, and representatives of the patriarchs of Antioch and Alexandria; more than 800 abbots and priors attended, plus representatives of the civil powers.

In the back of his mind, Innocent had the hope of another crusade to free the Holy Land. The first such crusade had begun in 1096 under Pope Urban II; for the next 175 years these attempts were repeated off and on. In each instance, there were, of course, political as well as religious considerations; but in no case was the Holy Land set free from the rule of the Saracens. What benefits the Crusades did bring to Europe were more indirect: the increase in scientific knowledge, commerce, art, and the like, which came from contact with the Arab nations.

Despite the earlier failures, Innocent III still hoped for one more such crusade. Thus, when the Council opened on November 11, 1215, the Pope first spoke, and then the patriarch of Jerusalem addressed the gathering; he was to describe the difficulties in the Holy Land. When the Council had concluded, a decree calling for a crusade was issued December 14, 1215. But Innocent III died in July of 1216, and with him the plans died also. The notion of a crusade was no longer appealing.

Of greater importance were the decrees of the second and third sessions of the Council, November 20 and 30. The IV Lateran Council issued the most important disciplinary legislation of the Middle Ages; it would not be equaled until the Council of Trent in the sixteenth century. There were the usual canons concerning the reform of the clergy and the proper education of those to be ordained. The most famous canon, however, was that which prescribed at least annual confession and Communion for all the faithful.

The greatest decrees were concerned with doctrine. The discussions of the early Scholastics were bearing fruit, and IV Lateran helped prepare the way for the great work of Thomas Aquinas (who was born ten years after the Council). This Council was the logical outgrowth of the great interest in doctrinal questions that marked the reign of Innocent III; many such concerns found expression chiefly in the canons pertaining to the sacraments.

One heretical teaching was condemned by adopting the very words of Peter Lombard, who had died in 1160 and was still considered *the* theologian of the day. A certain Abbot Joachim represented the results of bad philosophy in the study of God. He had made use of the more abstract words of philosophy to discuss the Trinity, but failed to express the truth adequately. He really ended up by holding that the three divine Persons were not actually one God; they were "one" only in a vague sense of being more or less joined together. This was not, however, the faith of the Church, as IV Lateran was careful to point out in repeating as its own the doctrine of Peter Lombard.

On the other hand, it was not only philosophers who had fallen into error. The Albigensian heresy (named after the city of Albi in southern France) took its rise among the more fanatical groups of simple Christians who set out to seek perfection apart from the Church. They were, in reality, following the same error as the Manichaeans at the time of St. Augustine. The material world came from the evil spirit; nonmaterial things came from God. The penances they performed were dictated more by a false notion of the body: since it is material, the body is evil; marriage is evil as well. This fanaticism began to spread on all sides; it was a religion that led only to despair, frustration. St. Dominic had begun to preach against this error at the start of the reign of Innocent III, about 1200; IV Lateran now spelled out officially the precise error the Church was fighting. This was done in the first canon, the so-called *Firmiter*, which is a detailed statement of the true Catholic belief; it is surely the most valuable statement of the Council.

IV Lateran also had to concern itself with one other group,

the Waldensians (named after Peter Waldo, who first became prominent about 1176). Peter Waldo was a rather devout layman, but one whose enthusiasm quickly led him to heresy. He and his followers — all laymen — felt called by God to preach, and they did so, even without the permission of the local bishops. Pope Alexander III had at once forbidden them to do this, but they continued. The movement then developed an anti-clerical and anti-Church spirit; priests and bishops were no more important than the laymen. In fact, the only thing that mattered was living a true apostolic life. If a man did that, he could forgive sins as well as a priest, or even better than some priests, since they concluded that a priest in the state of sin could not absolve.

This was, again, a faint foretaste of the Protestant spirit of the sixteenth century, which identified the spiritual powers of the visible Church with the weakness of the men who act as God's instruments. These Waldensians had been opposed earlier, and the IV Lateran Council included in its work a number of decrees aimed against them and similar movements.

As had been the case in the past, the directives of the IV Lateran Council failed to achieve fully the goals envisioned. They did, however, set the pattern for the difficulties which still lay ahead. Actually, this ought not seem especially surprising. Christ Himself had promised difficulties for His Church, and had foretold that not only the wheat but also the weeds would flourish in this earthly body. The Church without spot is the Church of the future. It is not surprising, then, if the Church must continue to fight; such is its destiny. The Church did not fail really. Its only failure would have been a refusal to fight, and these Councils of the Lateran are lasting evidence of the continuing struggle of Christ's Church against the weakness of its members. In its present state, the Body of Christ is waging a warfare. It is still very much the Church *militant*.

THE question of reform remained a chief concern of the Church during the years following IV Lateran, but the history of the Councils focuses attention on another recurring difficulty: the struggle of the Church with temporal rulers. In 1215, Frederick II (already king of Sicily and Puglia) became emperor of Germany. By 1220 he had managed to be solemnly crowned by Pope Honorius III. His grandfather, Frederick Barbarossa, had been a problem to Pope Alexander III and the III Lateran Council. Frederick II was now to prove an even greater burden to three later popes. But this struggle with the Hohenstaufen rulers was destined to come to a head under Pope Innocent IV. The I Council of Lyons (1245) stands as a witness to the strength of this Pope in resisting the power of temporal rulers who would challenge the spiritual rule of the Church.

Frederick soon after showed that he was going to be no special friend of the Church. His ultimate aim could be nothing more than to make the Church a part of the State. He had no regard for former promises and did all he could to obstruct the work of the Church. The popes, on the other hand, withstood him and emerged from the battle victorious. The man who had been

Frederick's tutor became Pope Honorius III in 1216. He was an old man by then, and hardly a match for the young prince who was beginning to show the crafty side of his nature. Honorius was much concerned about the situation in the Holy Land, and he had hoped for another crusade. Earlier, Frederick had promised to set out on such a crusade, but he never did. He later came into even closer conflict with the Pope. Honorius saw the conflict brewing, but he died in 1227 before it became an open battle.

The next pope was Gregory IX, a man who had served under Honorius III. He recognized the situation that had developed, and he had the strength to act at once. Gregory almost immediately excommunicated the Emperor for his failure to keep his promises, especially for his halfhearted attempts to fulfill his crusader's vow. Frederick ignored the Pope, however, and set out to cement his relations with the Mohammedan rulers of the East.

Something of an uneasy peace eventually dominated the reign of Gregory IX for some years, while Frederick did his best to gain control of as much territory as he could. By 1239, however, the Pope's patience gave way, and he again excommunicated the Emperor. Gregory also attempted to convoke a Council in 1241 to deal with Frederick. Knowing the difficulty of traveling through land so greatly controlled by the Emperor, the Pope arranged to have the bishops brought to Rome by the fleet of Genoa. The Emperor attacked the fleet, however, and captured 100 or more of the bishops and delegates.

It seemed that nothing would stop Frederick's new plans to take Rome. As he neared the city Gregory IX, now an old man, died; this was in August of 1241. By October 25, the few cardinals left had agreed on Celestine IV; and by November 10 he had died also. The choice now passed to Pope Innocent IV, although he was not elected for another year and a half, when

Louis IX of France managed to get Frederick to agree to release the cardinals he held as prisoners, and allow the election to continue.

Innocent IV was elected on June 25, 1243. He knew by now that there could be no compromise with Frederick. Either the Church became a department of the State, or Frederick would continue to fight until he made it that. On the other hand, the new Pope knew that, judging from experience, it would not be easy to outwit the Emperor. Nevertheless he set about making his plans carefully, with grim determination.

In May of 1244 he created twelve new cardinals; there were only nine left by now. He then transferred himself and his court to Lyons, in France. He had determined to convoke a General Council to deal with Frederick, and he knew this could not be done in Rome. He presumably did not make any agreement with the King of France concerning this move, although he was surely not ignorant of the fact that this saintly king (St. Louis) would be nearby in case help was needed. He chose Lyons as a more or less "free city." The French influence was strong, but it was still independent, and was not strictly within the empire of Frederick II. The city had the added advantage of being centrally located; it had been an important center in the ancient Roman Empire in Gaul.

Innocent then installed himself in the fortresslike monastery of St. Just at the beginning of December, 1244, and made arrangements for the Council. He set the opening for the feast of St. John the Baptist, June 24, 1245. In January of that year, he sent out his letters to the bishops and Christian princes. The purpose of the Council was obviously to deal with the Emperor, but the general concern with reform and with the threat of the Mohammedans also figured in his plans.

To clarify his position, Innocent IV once again excommunicated the Emperor on April 13, 1245, and on April 18 cited him to appear before the Council. At the beginning of June, Frederick wrote the cardinals protesting the action of the Pope; nevertheless he indicated that he would send his representatives to the gathering. In June the bishops began to arrive at Lyons — about 150, plus a good number of abbots.

There was a preparatory meeting two days later than the date planned for the opening of the Council. On June 26, the Pope met with Frederick's representatives in the refectory of the monastery. They proposed new conditions of peace, but the Pope would have none of it. The time for diplomacy and compromise was past. Frederick had shown that he could not be trusted and that he was intent on making the Church a department of the State. Innocent IV was determined that the matter should now be cleared up, once and for all.

The first solemn session opened in the Cathedral of St. John on June 28; the second and third sessions followed on July 5 and 17. Innocent himself preached at the opening session, comparing to the five wounds of Christ the five problems which grieved him: (1) the evil conduct of the bishops, the priests, and the faithful; (2) the onslaughts of the followers of Mohammed in the Holy Land; (3) the Greek schism; (4) the cruelty of the Tartars who had invaded Hungary; (5) the persecution of the Church by Frederick II. There was no doubt, however, that this Council had been called almost as a solemn trial of the Emperor. Frederick had been unfaithful in all ways, had attacked the Church, had held bishops captive, and had negotiated with the Mohammedans. He ought now be deposed as Emperor, since he had shown himself unworthy of this Christian office.

Basically this was a question of the relationship of the Church and State in the Middle Ages. It touched upon the question of whether any temporal ruler can dominate the Church, and whether the Christian people owe allegiance to a ruler who scorns the rights of the Church of Christ. All those who attended the Council realized from the start the true import of the discussions.

Frederick II was represented chiefly by Thaddeus of Suessa, the Archbishop of Palermo. He tried every line of argument. At first he suggested that it was not fair to try the Emperor without at least hearing him. This seemed to meet with agreement, and a delay of ten days was granted. Pope Innocent may not have been too enthused about Frederick appearing, most likely with his troops. Although he probably never said it, he is sometimes quoted as remarking: "I feel neither fit nor prepared either for prison or for martyrdom." This statement sums up the general fear felt by all.

The Emperor, however, indicated that he had no intention of appearing, so that the second session took place before the ten days were up. By this time, Frederick had lost whatever support he had had from the bishops. On July 5, he was accused of being contumacious and rebellious against the Church; a number of bishops rose to elaborate on the brutality of Frederick which they themselves had experienced. This time Frederick's representative, Thaddeus, insisted that the Emperor was on his way, and there should be a delay; he was really fighting for time. Thus the third session was postponed until July 17.

Actually Frederick had never left Verona, where he was; and he had no intention of leaving. Therefore, by the 17th all the papers were in order, and the Council proceeded to the condemnation. Thaddeus finally played his last card. He stated that if the condemnation took place, the Emperor would simply appeal to the next Pope and to a General Council, adding that this was no such Council. This brought forth a solemn statement on the part of Innocent that it *was* an Ecumenical Council, and the deposition took place. The decree stated that Frederick was deprived of his empire and his kingdoms, and excommunicated from the Church; all Christians were forbidden to obey him.

Innocent IV had exercised the full rights given to him by the social and political situation of the Middle Ages. The day of judgment had descended. Although we know little of them, it seems that the Council also issued a number of other canons; they dealt with the questions mentioned in the opening address of Innocent IV in the first session. With the singing of a solemn *Te Deum* the Council ended. The Dominicans and Franciscans were assigned the task of making known to the faithful the decision reached.

The Council was a great victory for the Church, at least in the realm of theory. The Church stood forth as the spiritual body that Christ intended it to be, free from the domination of temporal rulers. The hopes for another crusade came to nothing; the few attempts to contact the Tartars were not fully successful. But the Council was a victory of the papacy over the king, of the "cold-blooded" Innocent (as he has been described) over the unruly ruler.

Frederick continued to oppose the Pope and the Council; he contended that they had no right to act as they did. In Frederick's theory, the Pope could only crown the Emperor, but he had no right to exercise this power over the faithful. He would have attacked Lyons, but the French king let it be known that, although they were still allies of a sort, he would have to fight against him. In addition, in June of 1247 Frederick's army suffered a great defeat at Parma. He died three years later, in December of 1250. Innocent IV returned to Italy at long last. After staying a year and a half at Perugia, he entered Rome in October, 1253.

There was to be another General Council at Lyons in this century, II Lyons (held in 1274). This Council would be concerned with the still unsolved question of the Greek schism, finally stabilized under Michael Cerularius. Since this is closer in spirit to the Council of Florence (1438–1445), we will pass over it for the present, and return to it in Chapter XIII.

Thirty-two years after the death of Frederick II, another emperor entered the scene, and in large measure his intrigues were responsible for the next General Council: the Council of Vienne (1311–1312). This emperor was Philip the Fair, a ruler who came into conflict with the strongest Pope of the thirteenth century — Boniface VIII.

In 1294, Celestine V resigned his office as pope; he was one of the relatively few popes who have done so. After five months he was convinced that he was not the man for the office. As his successor the cardinals chose a man who knew his way in the world of diplomacy, and it was a fortunate choice. Just nine years before, Philip the Fair had become the new French king. He was a man who would tax the patience of the papacy. Much of what took place was not the result of what Boniface VIII himself had done; he inherited a difficult situation. He was, however, a strong-minded pope in addition to being a diplomat, and when he found himself involved in a quarrel with Philip, he fought ably.

At the beginning Boniface attempted to settle the difficulties by way of compromise; he possibly came out second best in this maneuver. His last years, therefore, showed a reawakened interest in proclaiming the spiritual independence of the Roman Pontiff. He left diplomacy aside, realizing that Philip was actually undermining the Church and supporting those fanatic Christians who were fast falling into heresy — the Spirituals and the Albigensians. The letter of December, 1301, written to the King indicated this new approach. It was entitled *Ausculta, Fili*, from its opening words: "Listen, O Son." It breathed the spirit of the medieval situation, in which even the Christian prince, as a member of the Church, was subject to the papal authority, and pointed out, accordingly, the effect of Philip's evil ways and bad example.

The King reacted violently to this approach, coached especially by his legal guide, Pierre Flotte. It was even suggested that Boniface was a heretic because of his pretensions; the ferment of Conciliarism was already at work in France. A gathering of bishops was held at Rome, and while there was no deposition of Philip as there had been of Frederick II, the most famous decree of Boniface's career did result — the *Unam sanctam* of November 18, 1302. It was above all a clear-cut statement of the authority of the Pope to correct the evil ways of all members of the Church, both high and low.

Although this decree did not mention either Philip or France, it was obviously aimed at him; he now continued his attacks on the Pope with even greater vehemence. In August of 1303 the Pope finally determined to excommunicate the King. Before he could do so publicly, the papal palace was stormed, and Boniface was threatened with prison or death. The aroused populace saved him for the day, but he was now an old man, about eighty; the situation was more than he could endure, and within three weeks he was dead.

The next pope, Benedict XI, continued the same line of approach in regard to the King, but when he seemed about to achieve lasting success, he died very suddenly; he had been pope for only nine months. The choice then fell on a French bishop who took the name of Clement V. He remained in France throughout his reign, and began the long line of men known as the Avignon popes which continued for nearly seventy-five years. He was crowned at Lyons in November of 1305.

Clement V was not the strong man that Boniface VIII had been. Yet, by his attitude toward the King, he did manage to avoid any complete break with him. On the other hand, Philip was still anxious to get even with what he considered the unjust intervention of Boniface VIII. In his new plans, he contemplated a condemnation of Boniface. To this he joined the hope of a condemnation of the Order of Knights Templar, to which he had lately turned his special attention.

For a time, considering the political and military strength of Philip, it appeared that some sort of trial of the dead Pope Boniface would take place; in fact, such a trial was already in the making. Pope Clement did manage to ward off any trial of Boniface; whatever records had already been made were destroyed. By way of compromise, it was agreed that the Order should be investigated, and the final decision regarding them sought from a General Council.

In this way the Council of Vienne (a few miles south of Lyons in France) came into existence. For many years, very little was known about the proceedings of this Council; even today our information is relatively scant. By a decree of April 4, 1310, Clement fixed the opening date of the Council for October 1 of the following year; actually the first solemn session did not take place until October 16, 1311. There were possibly 300 who attended in all, but the number of bishops was smaller. For the first time, a Pope *selected* the bishops who were to attend. Clement's list of 231 names was later reduced to about 165 under the order of the King, and not all of these attended.

We know that the principal task of the Council was the question of the Order of Knights Templar. There was also a discussion of help for the Holy Land and questions of doctrine and morals. We come to our knowledge of the doctrinal decrees, some of them quite important, only by a study of the official decrees themselves; we still know little about the actual sessions.

After the Council began with the solemn session on October 16, 1311, nothing more was done officially until the following spring; Philip himself arrived only on March 20. In the meantime, the Council reviewed, among other things, the records of the investigations of the Order of Knights Templar. This had been going on since 1307, and history has recorded the brutality of the inquiries carried on by the King.

This Order had been founded in the early part of the twelfth century; it was an outgrowth of the Crusades, and was originally dedicated to protecting the Christian pilgrims from attack. It had a strong military flavor, and many of the Knights had died in battle. The three vows of poverty, chastity, and obedience were also taken, so that it was a true religious order. In time, however, the Order had acquired large holdings, and thus became a powerful and a wealthy group. Philip had every reason to fear it.

The charge levied, however, was that this Order had been guilty of all sorts of crime. Its members supposedly denied Christ, dishonored the cross, practiced unnatural vice. The Grand Master, Jacques de Molay, had been arrested along with the other members, and they had confessed to all these crimes. History today passes a more mild judgment upon them than historians of the past. Without affirming that all the Knights were saints, it seems far more accurate to say that a good amount of torture was inflicted upon the members; they confessed to anything under these circumstances.

Pope Clement had agreed that the General Council would review all of this evidence. In the session of April 3 the final decision came forth: the Order would be suppressed, "for the good of the Church. . . ." With no further discussion, Clement and the Council solved this debate. It would seem that the Order was something of a peace offering. No particular Order is essential to the life of the Church; the Jesuits would also be suppressed for a time due to the political intrigues of the eighteenth century. In this instance, it seemed the most prudent decision under the circumstances. The large holdings of the Order, however, did not go to Philip, had he entertained any such hopes; they were given to the Hospitallers, a similar type of military order (or, in Spain, to national orders that had fought against the Moors).

The third session of May 6 was apparently concerned with doctrinal questions. One decree concerned the errors of Peter Olivi, although he is not mentioned by name. He had been a leader of a group of Franciscan monks known as the Spirituals, and had apparently fallen into error on certain points concerning Christ. In this decree the Council made its famous statement concerning the relationship of the human soul to the body.

Throughout this entire period of history, there were other movements that are difficult to identify as well-organized groups; they represent more of an attitude or an approach to Christianity. Among the Franciscans, the so-called Spirituals represented this attitude within religious life. These tendencies, however, led to so great an emphasis upon the inner life of man and the working of the Holy Spirit, that these people failed to give the necessary attention to the visible nature of the Church. The attachment to the spirit of poverty had led to criticism of the possessions of the Church, despite the fact that a visible Church must obviously possess certain material goods; but this criticism was not far from indicating a purely spiritual or invisible Church of Christ. Their interest was also centered on a scriptural theme that frequently preoccupied the medieval mind: the second coming of Christ, which was thought to be very near at hand.

At the Council of Vienne, the bishops had turned their attention to this general line of thought. As for the Spirituals, things were put in order rather soon under the next pope, John XXII (1316–1334). There were, however, far more radical groups of laymen and laywomen who had adopted some of this spirit; they were a source of great concern. We speak of them today as the Beghards and the Beguines (the first being the group of men; the second, the group of women). These were associations of pious people who did not take religious vows but who banded together to promote their spiritual perfection; they often engaged in special works of mercy as well. Some of these people, however, became interested in a type of spirituality not in keeping with the traditional teaching of the Church. While a large number of true "mystics" appeared in the Church during the thirteenth and fourteenth centuries, these people marked a decidedly false mysticism. This has been a recurring problem in the history of the Church, and the condemnation of these groups at Vienne indicates how far they had wandered from the truth.

Instead of following the general norms of prayer and fasting as means of drawing closer to God, these people so stressed "inner union with God," that the external practices became unimportant. They held that every man is blessed, and that he need not wait for heaven to "see" God; that is possible on earth. In this way, man can achieve such perfection during this life that he is entirely one with God; he no longer needs to pray or fast, since these are only *means* to the goal, and this man has now reached that goal.

Even more, because of his great perfection and his union with God, this "perfect man" can no longer sin. This is a teaching that reappeared in the Quietism of the seventeenth century; the name indicates the basic principle: "Let God act, and remain quiet under the hand of God." It is a belief that man need not concern himself with striving for perfection; if he "opens himself to God," nothing more is required. God alone will make him perfect.

Reduced to a more practical level, this teaching had also concluded that man need not concern himself with temptation and sin. Provided he adheres to God, he cannot sin. The Beg-hards and Beguines even concluded that if one follows the promptings of nature in regard to sex, there could be no sin; perfection would not interfere with this. In fact, the "spiritual" man is so perfect that he can allow free reign to his fleshly desires.

It is more than obvious why the Council of Vienne was called upon to condemn these teachings. These were most serious matters. In its condemnations, the Council gives us an insight into the problems of the age. In some of them, especially the criticism of the possessions of the Church and the tendency to emphasize an invisible Church, we can see already the faint outline of the teachings of the Protestant Revolt in the sixteenth century. Before this revolt, however, another crisis faced the Church — the so-called Western Schism. This dispute between the contenders for the papal throne was solved by what is perhaps the most unusual of all the General Councils, the Council of Constance in 1414.

CHAPTER XII ... *Council of Constance*

WHEN the disputes between the popes and the emperors had somewhat died down, a new scandal fell upon the Church in the fourteenth century. After almost 75 years in Avignon, in 1377 the papacy returned to Rome permanently under Gregory XI. This was an important move, and there was much to be done in order to re-establish the papal court in the Eternal City. Gregory XI accomplished little in this regard, however, for in March of 1378 he died, and the confusion that resulted afterward continued to plague the Church for almost forty years.

When Gregory XI died, the people of Rome were most insistent that the new pope be elected immediately and in Rome itself; they also wanted a Roman, or at least an Italian pope. As a result, the cardinals then present in Rome proceeded to elect the first Italian pope in almost 75 years, even though they were mostly French cardinals. The man elected was the Archbishop of Bari; he chose the name of Urban VI. The election was a joy to the Italian populace, but it soon proved a burden to the cardinals. By September, even the few Italian cardinals had become discontent under the harshness of this admittedly tactless Pope.

Then a most unheard of thing took place. After much secret planning, the cardinals left Rome and gathered at Anagni. There they announced that the election of Urban was invalid, since pressure had been brought to bear upon them. Soon after they elected a second "pope," Clement VII, as he called himself. This marks the beginning of the Great Western Schism.

It is generally agreed today that there was no reason for calling the election of Urban VI invalid; it had followed all the prescribed norms. Under these circumstances, however, there was great confusion. Today, far from the fracas, we can more calmly single out the true Pope. At the time, there were many who judged the reports to be true, and who therefore accepted Clement VII as the true Pope. On the other hand, there were Catholics who continued to accept Urban VI as the validly elected Pope. The end result was a split in the Christian world that would last from 1378 until 1417.

The difficulty was not whether the Church had a Pope or not; it was simply a question of who he was. Many sincere people, even some of the saints, were confused and supported the wrong man. As a result, as each contestant died, a successor was elected by the cardinals who supported him; thus a line of popes was established on each side. Today we speak of the "Roman Line," which represents the true popes, following Urban VI; and the "Avignon Line," indicating Clement VII and the man who succeeded him, who eventually installed themselves as pope at Avignon:

Roman Line	*Avignon Line*
Urban VI (1378–1389)	Clement VII (1378–1394)
Boniface IX (1389–1404)	Benedict XIII (1394–1417)
Innocent VII (1404–1406)	
Gregory XII (1406–1415)	

Confusion was multiplied even more as both of these men

continued to name bishops and cardinals, to assign them to various dioceses, and to punish or excommunicate certain members of both parties. Obviously, of course, only the true Pope had the right to do these things; but no one was sure which one he was — perhaps not even the antipopes themselves.

In time, voices were raised, especially at the University of Paris, suggesting that the schism could be solved only by having the two men resign, and electing a new pope at a General Council. This was ultimately to be the solution of the problem, but it was not an unmixed blessing. Underneath this there was being formulated the teaching of "Conciliarism," that is, that a General Council is superior to the Pope. This would destroy the nature of the Church established by Christ on Peter. We describe the Church as a monarchical society; this means the rule of one man, above all, serving as the vicar of Christ. The Conciliar Theory would subject the vicar of Christ to the power of a General Council.

The Avignon Pope at times began to consider accepting these plans, but he died before any results were achieved. Immediately a successor was elected, Benedict XIII. Although he was not the true pope, Benedict at least withstood the moves of the Conciliar Party. He and Gregory XII became the leading figures of what seemed to be a solution to the schism.

For a time it had seemed as though a meeting of the two parties could be arranged and an agreement reached. But the preparations proved futile. Political maneuvers abounded on all sides. The next step only added to the already existing confusion. Growing more and more disgruntled with the proceedings in both parties, the majority of cardinals on both sides agreed to abandon both of the contending Popes, and meet in a Council that would attempt to solve this problem. If the two men would not abdicate, they would be deposed by this Council, and a new pope elected.

This meeting actually took place at Pisa in 1409, apart from both Popes, and it resulted in the election of still another Pope. He took the name of Alexander V; he is the first of the so-called "Pisan Line." He lived less than a year, and was succeeded by another antipope, John XXIII. Pisa had been a great and well-attended gathering, but it marked a high point in the Conciliar Movement. The cardinals from both parties had met and acted without papal confirmation, accepting the theory that a General Council is superior to the Pope.

There were now *three* men, all claiming to be the lawful vicar of Christ. The final solution came through the Council of Constance. Despite all the confusion and misunderstanding that surrounded it, this gathering ranks as an Ecumenical Council of the Church. If ever the Holy Spirit managed to exert His influence in the Church through the most unlikely of instruments, it was through this Council.

A new figure entered the scene at this stage: Sigismund of Luxemburg, who was elected King of the Romans in 1411. He came to Italy to arrange a Council with the antipope John XXIII (who had held a rather badly attended Council in Rome in 1412). Sigismund insisted on Constance as the city where the sessions should be held; John XXIII gave way to his wishes.

The result is a peculiar situation from our point of view. The Council of Constance was first set in motion by the Emperor and a man who was not actually the true Pope! The truth is, however, that all three "Popes" at some time came into contact with this Council; all agreed in some manner to its proceedings; and Martin V, who was to emerge from the Council as the next pope, approved most of the decrees of the Council. Thus it was a General Council of the universal Church, even though some of the decrees issued were out-and-out heresy; these decrees were rejected by later popes. In this, the gathering was not unlike some of the earlier Councils, which also got out of hand, and were approved only in part by the Roman Pontiff. But like them, this Council remained a General Council in the proper sense of the word in those matters which were approved by the head of the body of bishops.

In October of 1413, Sigismund announced to the Christian world that the Council would open on November 1, 1414. In December of that year John XXIII, who was at Lodi, issued a bull of convocation. At that time, John XXIII had many followers, although his cause would later collapse.

John XXIII arrived at Constance toward the end of October, 1414. The city lies along the Lake of Constance, a northern city, but one then outside the French rule. The Council was declared to be opened on November 1 of that year, although the first solemn session did not take place until November 16. On the following day, the 17th, Peter d'Ailly, the cardinal bishop of Cambrai, arrived. He was, in large measure, the "soul" of the entire gathering, even though his own views were more than tainted with the error of Conciliarism. In December, Sigismund also reached the city. In number, about 300 bishops and abbots attended, together with a large number of theologians and canon lawyers. It is almost impossible, however, to determine the exact number associated with this rather drawn-out Council.

Of the three men then looked upon as "Pope," all had more or less agreed to resign the office in the interests of the peace of the Church. John XXIII has been greatly discussed by later biographers, perhaps even calumniated; but he was far from the spiritual type of ecclesiastic. Nevertheless, he did recognize the need for a solution, and despite the confusion he caused, he remained more or less faithful to his agreement. He regarded himself as the lawful pope, of course; he based his claim on the action of the Council at Pisa.

Gregory XII, whom we recognize today as the lawful pope, was about 87 years old. He was most insistent that he remain pope, but agreed that he would resign if need be. As his condition for so doing, he stipulated that John XXIII must not be accepted as the true pope at all. The Avignon pope, Benedict XIII, preferred to deal directly with the Emperor; in the long run, this man may have been the least co-operative. He had retired to Spain, and had avoided all earlier attempts at reunion.

From the start, it was obvious to the Council that the only possible solution was to have all three contestants resign and elect another man. This would mean, of course, that the lawful Pope would have to give up his office along with the other two; but this had been done before, and was perfectly in accord with the laws of the Church.

There were some objections from the cardinals who had taken part in the discussions at Pisa; they wanted the Council of Constance to recognize this gathering and its decisions. Peter d'Ailly managed to convince them that this was not the prudent thing to do; it would only cause greater doubts and confusion. The address in which he accomplished this feat was overloaded with errors of a conciliar nature; but fortunately the main goal was achieved, and the matter was dropped.

By January of 1415, the support enjoyed by John XXIII began to falter. There were at first rather hidden attacks upon him and his office; he had insisted all along that the Council recognize him as the lawful pope. Finally the suggestion was brought out into the open that all three, including John, would have to resign. About the same time, word reached the Council that both Gregory XII and Benedict XIII were agreeable to such a plan; it was apparent to John that he also would have to oblige. He was not pleased, however. At first he offered to make a public confession of his faults; the offer was rejected, and on March 1, 1415, John solemnly promised to resign if the other two did likewise.

Benedict XIII had asked for negotiations to take place elsewhere in his regard; the Emperor agreed to this. There was some fear, however, that the Council might break up. Sigismund, however, refused to allow anyone to leave Constance. He insisted that the Council remain together until its task was accomplished. Shortly after that, strange to say, John himself escaped from Constance during the excitement of a tournament, disguised as a stableman. From Schaffhausen he did write to the Council, informing them that he would still stand by his promises.

This act of John upset those at Constance, of course; this time, it was Sigismund who kept them all there. A delegation was sent to John, but everything he said continued to annoy those taking part in the gathering. It is significant that during these days the bishops formulated the now famous "Articles of Constance," the heretical statements, declaring that a General Council is superior to the Pope. These were approved in the fourth and fifth sessions (March 30 and April 6, 1415). The vote was taken up according to nations, as had been previously agreed. This had been one of the perplexing problems of the Council. To allow each individual a vote might have permitted a majority from a larger country to control the decisions. As a result, the nations voted in one bloc: the Italians, Germans, French, English, and somewhat later the Spanish. What was agreed on by the nations (*nationaliter*) would then be set forth solemnly by the Council (*conciliariter*).

Between April 17 and May 29 the formula of abdication for John XXIII was drawn up and he was solemnly deposed. He was invited to come back to the Council; he chose to send his representatives. They could accomplish nothing in his behalf, so that at the tenth session, John was declared suspended, and at the twelfth session (May 29) he was solemnly deposed. John was, by now, a broken man; he accepted the decree with no protest. He was kept under guard nearby. Later, after Martin V had been elected the new pope, John returned to union with him. He died in 1419 as a cardinal under Martin V. Since he was not the true pope, the present pontiff assumed the name John XXIII when he was elected in 1958.

What some of the members of the Council may have *thought* they were doing is an interesting question. Many were surely convinced that they were deposing the lawful Pope; this was the man they had accepted as such. Their conciliar notions led them to such an action. In point of fact, however, they had not deposed the Pope; there was only one true vicar of Christ. It was, then, to Gregory XII that the Council now turned its attention.

It is both interesting and important to note that Gregory insisted to the end that he was the only lawful pope, and that everything done by the Council was accomplished in a manner that would safeguard his claims. In January, 1415, the delegates of Gregory had notified the Council of his willingness to abdicate; in June of that year, his representatives arrived at Constance, empowered to act with full authority in his name.

These representatives first went to the Emperor, since Gregory did not admit this as a lawful Council. Because of this position, the Emperor acceded to their desires and presided at the fourteenth session (July 4, 1415). The representatives thereupon read the abdication of Gregory, and also the decree which authorized them to convoke this Council, by reason of the resignation; it was accordingly authorized to act as a General Council and proceed to the election of a new pope. Gregory had taken this step "for the union and the reform of the Church, and to destroy heresy." He died two years later, October 18, 1417.

The problem of Benedict XIII had to be solved before a new pope could be elected. This required more negotiating. Benedict did finally agree to give up his claims, but only on the condition that all of the sentences levied against him be removed, especially those issued by the gathering at Pisa. In February of 1416 the Council ratified this agreement; in October of that year, Spain was granted its vote along with the other nations. Not until July 26, 1417, however, were all the preliminaries finished; the final decree was then accepted, deposing Benedict.

The final problem was the election of a new pope, and this also brought forth disagreements. There was first of all the question of who ought to elect him. For over 350 years, only cardinals had been entrusted with this task; yet some did not trust the cardinals after all these experiences. In addition, the Emperor wanted the Council to decree reforms at once, before the election; most of the cardinals, however, insisted that the new pope be chosen first. The problem had begun to be discussed in June of 1417, even before Benedict XIII had been deposed. By October, a compromise was reached, mostly through the efforts of the English Cardinal, Henry Beaufort.

The Council would first declare that as soon as the Pope was elected, the matter of Church reform had to be treated; at the same time, it would immediately issue a list of reforms on which all were now agreed; and finally, a special commission would be established to determine the manner in which the pope should be elected.

Of the decrees issued at this time, the most famous is the *Frequens,* which established the need of frequent Councils. One was to be held five years after Constance, the next one seven years after that, and then every ten years. Another decree provided that if a schism should occur again, a Council would meet within the year to settle the question.

It was finally decided that the twenty-three cardinals would take part in the election, along with thirty other delegates (six from each of the five nations); this procedure would hold true only for this election. So it was that, after a short conclave of three days, Martin V appeared as the new and undisputed Pope on November 11, 1417. Questions of reform and the new matter of concordats (or agreements) with the nations occupied the Council until it finally ended on April 22, 1418; this was in the forty-fifth session, some three and a half years after the Council began.

The most important work of the Council was naturally the ending of the schism and the election of a new pope. The problems related to this, however, continued to trouble the Church in the years that followed. The conciliar notions had not yet died out, and it was the uneasy task assigned to Martin V to weave in and out of the maze of difficulties without upsetting things and causing a new schism; the independent spirit that had caused these problems was unfortunately not smothered by his election.

Pope Martin V approved the acts of the Council, with the exception of those which proposed Conciliarism. Some have questioned whether this was really a General Council because of the difficulties involved, but in the light of many earlier Councils, there should be no doubt. The sessions which took place after Martin V had been elected raise no problem at all, but his acceptance of the earlier decisions would be sufficient to make them of equal force.

Among the other decrees of the Council, the most important were the condemnations of the teachings of John Wyclif and John Hus. Wyclif had died in 1384, but his teaching was still alive. He had been an Oxford theologian, condemned in England in 1382. In that same year, the English King had married the sister of the King of Bohemia, thus opening an exchange of interest and ideas between the two countries. One of the results of this union was that the teaching of Wyclif gradually found its way to Prague, where, about the beginning of the fifteenth century, it captured the mind of John Hus (1370–1415), the rector of the University of Prague and a well-known preacher.

The doctrine of Wyclif and of Hus is surprisingly like that which is to appear a hundred years later at the time of the Protestant Revolt; it is an important indication that the mentality which formed the Revolt was already being created long before the time of Luther. Wyclif had challenged the visible structure of the Church, rejected the Sacrifice of the Mass, and emphasized Scripture as the sole rule of faith.

Wyclif, as we have said, was dead at the time of the Council of Constance; thus only his doctrine was condemned. Hus, however, was brought to Constance and condemned for teaching the errors of Wyclif; he had already been excommunicated by the Archbishop of Prague and then by the antipope, John XXIII. The Council declared him a heretic, and when he refused to reject these beliefs, he was handed over to the civil authorities for execution. This was the manner of dealing with all heretics at the time; as late as 1553 the Geneva Calvinists would inflict the same penalty in the famous case of Michael Servetus, who had attacked the doctrine of the Trinity. The death of Hus, however, became something of a national symbol in Bohemia where his followers formed the Hussite party.

Among his many problems, Martin V was still faced with the question of Conciliarism, and it is this that leads us to the next General Council. The Council of Constance decreed that a General Council should be held five years after the close of this gathering, i.e., in 1423 — the worst possible time for a Council. Wars were raging on all sides, and it was soon apparent that few bishops would be able to attend. Nevertheless, Martin arranged for a Council to open at Pavia in April of that year; in June the plague struck in Pavia and the legates moved the gathering to Siena. It was not until November that enough bishops were present for any kind of Council; even at that, there were only about twenty-five. The discussions which did take place indicated the danger that was still very much present:

Conciliarism. Nothing was accomplished by this feeble effort, and in March of 1424 the legates dissolved the Council, agreeing to hold the next gathering at Basel in 1431 (seven years later, as stipulated at Constance).

Pope Martin V had come through safely with one "required" Council; not enough bishops attended nor enough was done to constitute a General Council. He would possibly have preferred no more Councils at all, and with good reason; the spirit of Conciliarism remained a constant threat to the peace of the Church. As the year 1431 approached, however, little notices were tacked on the papal walls, reminding him and the people of the need to proclaim the next Council. The implications were clear enough: if he failed to do so, others could convoke the Council for him. Again Martin decided it was better to go along with the plans, in the hope of keeping the gathering under control. He announced the next Council in February of that year, but he died three weeks later.

The next pontiff, Eugene IV, confirmed the decree summoning the Council at Basel, in Switzerland. Once more, the gathering got off to a bad start; hardly anyone showed up. In July, the discussions started, but the hall was still almost empty. As more and more delegates did arrive matters started to get confused. On December 14, 1431, the first session was held, but at that very moment, a decree was on its way from Rome, empowering the legates to dissolve the Council; four days later a second document was signed by Eugene actually dissolving it. The reports he had received indicated that this might well become another unruly gathering; his fears were not unfounded.

Regardless of what the spirit had been from the start, the bishops who had gathered at Basel were angered when they heard that the Pope had dissolved the Council. They reissued the heretical decrees of Constance, stating once again that the General Council is superior to the Pope, and that he has no power to dissolve such a gathering.

This series of misunderstandings continued. For a time it seemed the Pope would once again enter into negotiations with the Council; but he refused to accept the decrees concerning the supremacy of a General Council. The disputes dragged on and on for years, always much the same. At long last, on January 1, 1438, Eugene IV gave up the practice of struggling for time by diplomacy and discussion, and ordered a fresh start at Ferrara.

This marked the final break. The bishops who embraced the Conciliar Theory refused to yield; they continued in open schism until 1449, electing once again an antipope. This time, however, they were clearly a minority. The position of Pope Eugene was stronger, and the Council he called at Ferrara was well attended: we speak of it today as the Council of Florence. Its main concern was to be an attempt at reunion with the Greek schismatics. During the calmer years at Basel, the first steps were taken to contact the Greeks in the hope of bringing them back to the Church. The discussions with the Greeks actually took place at Ferrara and Florence.

Strangely, the world was now faced with the spectacle of not only two popes again, but of two contending Councils. But this time there was to be no repetition of the Great Western Schism. What was done at Basel had no lasting effect. Basel was never recognized as a General Council, although in later disputes with the Roman Pontiff the heretical decrees of both Constance and Basel were cited as definitions of the Church; this was especially true in the so-called Gallican Liberties affirmed in the seventeenth century by a large body of French clergy.

As had happened often in the past, out of much confusion the Holy Spirit managed to set forth clearly and firmly the unchanging truth. Not only was the immediate problem solved, but the doctrine concerning the papacy was greatly clarified. Today, the role of the vicar of Christ is perceived more clearly because of the unruly disputes carried on during this period of the Church's life.

CHAPTER XIII . . . *II Lyons — Florence*

EVER since the eleventh century, the problem of reunion with the East has been a special concern of the Church. The Council of Florence in the fifteenth century stands as a testimony to this concern. Before going on with a discussion of this gathering, however, we ought to turn back the wheels of time for a momentary consideration of a similar attempt in the thirteenth century — II Lyons. Both of these Councils failed to achieve the goal sought, but they did witness the desire of Rome for such reunion. In addition, they resulted in our clearest doctrinal statements regarding the Holy Spirit as the third Person of the Trinity.

After a vacancy of nearly three years following the death of Clement IV, Pope Gregory X was finally elected in September of 1271. He was crowned at Rome in March of 1272, and he immediately announced the convocation of a General Council. He later named Lyons in France as the city where the Council would be held.

As with the Lateran Councils of the twelfth and thirteenth centuries, II Lyons was to be concerned with the need of reform within the Church. In calling it, Gregory was also troubled about the loss of a large part of the Holy Land as well as with what this implied — the continuing progress of Mohammedan belief. This non-Christian religion was a constant threat to the Christian world during these ages, both politically and religiously. If the Turks conquered the West, both the Christian faith and Western civilization would be seriously challenged.

Gregory's special concern, however, was for reunion with the Greeks. As soon as he called the Council, he notified Joseph, the patriarch of the Greeks, of his intention. At the same time, he communicated with Michael VIII Paleologus, the Greek Emperor, inviting him to attend either personally or through his legates (granted full power to act in his name).

The Pope had chosen Lyons as the city for the Council because he himself had been a canon of Lyons, and had also taken part in I Lyons; hence he knew its resources for such a gathering. By way of preparation, he named five new cardinals who would play important roles at the gathering. Among them was the then bishop of Lyons, Peter of Tarentaise (later Pope Innocent V), and St. Bonaventure, the Superior-General of the Franciscans.

The Pope himself arrived in November of 1273 to preside, and soon afterward the other members of the Council gathered. II Lyons is noteworthy for the personages who did attend. In addition to Pope Gregory himself, three future popes were present and another was active in the preparations; St. Bonaventure and St. Albert the Great were both present, and eventually the representatives of the Greek Emperor also appeared. St. Thomas Aquinas was to have attended, but he died on the way to the Council. In all, about 500 bishops and cardinals attended together with more than 1000 other members of the clergy. While the Pope actually presided, the dominant role was played by St. Bonaventure and Peter of Tarentaise.

The Council opened officially on May 7, 1274, in the Cathedral

Church of St. John. The Pope spoke of the three-fold purpose of the Council: reunion with the Greeks, general reform, and the problem of the Holy Land. Early in the proceedings word came that the legates of the Greeks were to attend. The second and third sessions (May 18 and June 7) were especially concerned with preparations for that meeting, but some disciplinary decrees were also formulated at that time.

The Greek representatives finally arrived at Lyons on June 24; among them were the patriarch of Constantinople himself and the metropolitan of Nicea. They met with the Pope and presented letters from the Emperor and the Greek prelates, testifying their willingness to accept the faith of Rome. On June 29, the feast of SS. Peter and Paul, the Pope celebrated a solemn Mass in the cathedral, during which the Epistle, Gospel, and *Credo* were chanted both in Latin and in Greek. In the *Credo,* the Greeks repeated three times, in their own language, the controversial phrase concerning the Holy Spirit: "Who proceeds from the Father and the Son" (*Qui ex Patre Filioque procedit*).

At the fourth session (July 6), there was a solemn profession of faith. George Acropolita, the special representative of Michael Paleologus, recited it in the name of the Emperor; the others did likewise, all accepting the primacy of the Roman Pontiff. A solemn *Te Deum* of thanksgiving was intoned by the Pope, sung both in Latin and in Greek. The work of reunion was apparently achieved. The Council then turned its attention to the remaining problems, above all the matter of papal elections. Gregory X wished to be sure that no three-year vacancy would ever recur; his suggestions, however, met with opposition. In the end, he won out, and it was decreed that the conclave should begin ten days after the Pope's death. Those present should remain until the Pope is elected, and to hurry them along, the regulation was added that if a Pope were not chosen in three days, only one dish is to be served for the cardinals' dinner and supper. If the election continued eight days, only bread, wine, and water should be served until the election is completed.

As for the hopes of reunion, they were stillborn. The break resulted largely from political considerations, and so also did the reunion; hence it could not be lasting. The third canon of I Constantinople and the twenty-eighth of Chalcedon had set the spirit of competition between Constantinople and Rome; Cerularius had brought the final break. While there were many, even in the thirteenth century, who did not think of it as a lasting break, nothing was done effectively to bridge the gap until Pope Gregory X. Politically, there was the fear that union with Rome would mean the end of the Eastern empire and the re-establishment of the Roman. Religiously, there were objections above all because of the *"Filioque"* ("... and the Son") which by now had become a major concern. The unwillingness of the Eastern patriarch to be considered anything less than an "equal" with the Roman Pontiff also entered into the picture.

Pope Urban IV and Pope Clement IV had both made some vague moves for reunion immediately before Gregory; they had been careful to insist, however, that a future Council would not be for debate, but for acceptance of the Roman faith. Despite this, one doctrine was discussed at II Lyons. The First Canon proclaimed that the Holy Spirit proceeded or came forth from the Father *and the Son* "as from one principle." There were not two eternal sources of the life of the third Person; the life of the Trinity was communicated to the Spirit by the Father and the Son as though from only one principle or source.

This manner of expression satisfied the Greek representatives; moreover, this was an important declaration of Catholic belief. Michael VIII Paleologus, however, had most probably consented to the Council more because of political motives than religious ones; he was fearful of Charles of Anjou, the king of Sicily, who threatened his power. Union with Rome was the one sure way of tying the hands of Charles.

In addition, the people of the East were strongly opposed to union with Rome for emotional reasons. When, after II Lyons, attempts were made to put the reunion into practice, the populace split violently into two parties — some in favor, some against. Above all, opposition arose among the monks, who were particularly influential with the people. A good number finally reached the position where they would rather see the kingdom perish than consent to destroy what they considered the purity of their faith by the "heresy of Rome."

From the Roman side, the change in popes during the years immediately following II Lyons hampered further success. As one writer comments, during these crucial years a series of popes passed over the papal throne like meteors; there were five popes between 1276 and 1285. This made it difficult to give stability to the plans.

As a result of this lack of success, relations cooled again between Rome and Constantinople. Paleologus had realized that union with Rome would not be the political help he had hoped for. Even though he continued diplomatic relations with Rome, he began arranging a military offensive against the West. All of this finally resulted in the excommunication of Paleologus by Pope Martin IV. The Emperor died in 1282. Under his son, Andronicus, the anti-Roman reaction took over completely, and the hopes of II Lyons were crushed entirely.

In the fifteenth century, a second fruitless attempt was made to secure union of the East and the West. As we have already noted in Chapter XII, this union had its first start at Basel, which resulted in a repetition of the worst days of Constance. The Council had its real start, then, at Ferrara in 1438, and later moved to Florence and finally to Rome.

When the Council of Constance (1414–1418) had cleared up

the papal schism and elected Martin V, there was still much to be accomplished in the way of reform. In fact, few popes had ever been elected with more perils at hand. The final acts of the Council of Constance gave rise to perhaps the most grave problem of all — the challenge to the primacy of the Roman Pontiff. As we have seen, this challenge did not die at Constance; it was revived at Basel, and continued to trouble the popes for many years.

When Eugene IV finally broke completely with the Council of Basel, he did so by a decree issued in January, 1438, transferring the Council to Ferrara, in Italy. Many bishops followed this decree; they set out for Ferrara, leaving behind a clearly schismatical group that continued its strivings for eleven more years.

The Council of Florence was in reality, a fresh start. It is divided into three periods: Ferrara (January 8, 1438 – January 10, 1439); Florence (February 26, 1439 – April 26, 1442); Rome (April 26, 1443 – August 7, 1445). Florence was a city more acceptable to the Greeks to begin with, and they were now on the way; they had at least insisted on some place in Italy for the meeting, so Ferrara would also have been acceptable.

As at II Lyons, unfortunately, we are faced here with conflicting motives. There was in the Western Church a sincere desire for religious union, shared by many in the East. The emperor, John VIII Paleologus, however, could feel the breath of the Turks on his neck, and, as at II Lyons, we can perceive politics and military security as the chief motive of the Emperor in agreeing to reunion with Rome. Many of the Greek bishops also failed to share this enthusiasm for reunion, but they went along with it. Some, in fact, had to — the Emperor eventually forbade them to speak against it any further.

The Roman Pontiff had arranged for the travel of the Greek delegates to Italy. They landed at Venice on February 8, 1438;

they reached Ferrara in early March. While waiting for them to arrive, the Western bishops had opened the Council as planned on January 8, 1438. There had been a number of preliminary sessions, suspending the schismatic group at Basel and making plans for the discussions with the Greeks.

Once they had landed in Venice, however, the division between the Greeks (as well as their extreme sensitiveness) became quite apparent. Even before they arrived, they seemed to have chosen their sides, for or against union. They also fell into minor disputes concerning the manner in which they ought to greet the Pope, the proper order of precedence among the bishops, and the ever recurring problem at this Council: the question of the financial reimbursement they were to receive.

They arrived at Ferrara in full splendor; the details of precedence were all solved somehow, but not without a great deal of fuss concerning the position of the various thrones and their respective heights. At last, on April 9, a truly fantastic picture was unveiled in the Church of St. George. The Latins gathered on the Gospel side, and the Greeks on the Epistle side. The Emperor was present, as well as his son, Demetrius (who happened to be against the idea of union). The Pope was there also, as well as Joseph II, the patriarch of Constantinople — a sick, old man who favored the union, and who had made this long journey for that reason, knowing full well that he would probably never return home.

Among the Latins the dominant figure was Cardinal Cesarini. For the Greeks, there was Bessarion, the archbishop of Nicea (who favored union from sincere motives), and Mark of Ephesus (violently opposed to it).

Never had the Western world seen such a magnificent gathering of personages as this. But then things came to a temporary halt. The Emperor was particularly upset because none of the Western princes had shown up; he could hardly satisfy his political and military plans if no one but disputing priests showed up. For this reason, nothing important was done for the next six months — until October 8, when the temporal princes arrived. The Emperor went hunting; the cardinals and bishops had dinners; and the financial resources for supporting them all ran lower and lower. Eventually a commission of theologians, half Latin and half Greek, was appointed to discuss the main problems: the Procession of the Holy Spirit, the use of unleavened bread, Purgatory, and the primacy of the Pope.

At long last, the first important session got under way on October 8, 1438, in the Pope's chapel; about 200 bishops took part in the proceedings of the Council. In all, sixteen sessions took place at Ferrara from that date until January 10, 1439. The situation was somewhat different from that adopted at II Lyons, for in this instance, the theological questions were debated openly, particularly that concerning the *"Filioque."*

While Photius and Cerularius had mentioned this question, it did not have the import with them that it later assumed; it was now very central. The II Council of Lyons had, of course, solved one principal objection: it defined that the Western Church held the Holy Spirit proceeded from the Father and the Son as "from one principle," and not from two distinct sources. This was a real concern for some of the sincere theologians of the East. Antiquity noted two phrases that had been used to explain this doctrine. Once Arianism had been conquered, all agreed that the Son proceeded from the Father; the attention now centered upon the eternal relationship of the Holy Spirit to these Two.

One phrase — used by some Latin writers, but favored in the *East* — stated that the Spirit proceeded "from the Father through the Son" (*ex Patre per Filium*). The other — used by some Greek writers, but favored in the *West* — stated that the Spirit proceeded from the Father "and the Son" (*Filioque* — *"que"* being the word for "and," attached to the end of the word for "Son"). Through the efforts of Bessarion and George Scholarios, a learned layman, the Greeks at Florence were convinced that the two phrases meant the same thing. A statement of this fact was incorporated into the final decree.

The argument continued, however, on a more technical point. The Council of Ephesus had decreed that no one could add anything to the Nicene Creed. Thus the Greeks insisted that the Church of Rome could not add the *"Filioque,"* and the Latins insisted that it could do so. In the background, of course, was the question of papal authority in doctrinal questions.

This particular point had been debated ever since the contact with Alcuin and other Western theologians who attended II Nicea as representatives of Charlemagne (787). The phrase was certainly added to the Creed, perhaps first of all in Spain; the practice then spread. The Greeks were fond of citing Pope Leo III who, at the beginning of the ninth century, refused to admit the phrase into the Creed as recited at Rome. His reason was actually the *addition,* rather than the teaching, although he was now quoted as also being against the doctrine expressed by the phrase.

With time, these problems were solved, but not at Ferrara. The plague had come to Ferrara, and this suggested a move. In addition, the Pope was no longer able to pay for the food, lodging, and wages associated with the Council. Robbers had continually interfered with delivery of funds from Rome. The people of Florence, however, agreed to undertake the support of the Council; and the Greeks, at first somewhat unwilling, agreed when it was stated that their back wages would be forthcoming in Florence.

At Florence, the Emperor apparently got tired of the priestly debates, and was sorry that no other princes came; his main desire now was to conclude a union and leave. Since this de-

manded unity among the Greek theologians, the Emperor
stepped in and silenced those against union (who were already
decreasing in number). This did not exactly rush matters, but
along with a new system of commissions that met separately
rather than in a full session, a final formula of union was worked
out. On June 8, 1439, the Greeks finally accepted the points
on the Procession of the Holy Spirit, and between then and
July 5, the other questions were discussed and acceptable
formulas devised.

The ailing patriarch, Joseph II, died on June 10. Some of
the other Greek bishops (as well as the learned layman, Scholarios) purposely left the Council about the same time, before
the solemn signing of the decree. One bishop stayed, stead-
fastly refusing to sign: Mark of Ephesus. This manner of avoid-
ing the question of signing the decree is quite significant in
view of what happened after the Council had ended.

When the time for the official signing arrived, the Greeks
gathered with the Emperor to place their signatures on the
final formula; this occurred on July 5, 1439. In all, thirty-three
Greek representatives signed. At the same time, the Latins met
with the Pope at the Church of St. Maria Novella, where one
hundred and seventeen more signed. The next day, the Pope
celebrated a solemn Mass in the Cathedral at Florence, where
the final decree was read aloud.

Soon after, the Emperor and the other Greek delegates were
on their way home. Certain matters were left unsolved — especially the election of a new patriarch, and the problem of what
to do when one city had two bishops, a Latin and a Greek.
(This was eventually solved according to which bishop died
first; the diocese then reverted to the other rite.)

The Council of Florence continued after the Greeks left, but
we know little about it. The schism at Basel had to be discussed,
and new requests came from other Oriental bishops seek-

ing union. The Armenians were on their way when the first decree was being formulated; they arrived as the Greeks were leaving. A formula of agreement was drawn up for them, although in practice nothing ever came of it; the situation had changed radically when their delegates returned home. In 1442, a similar decree was issued for the Jacobites, sent by the King of Ethiopia; again it was not of lasting value.

As with II Lyons, the Council of Florence failed to achieve a lasting union. The mixed motives involved in achieving a formula of union could not be overcome. Of the Eastern rites now in union with Rome (the so-called *Uniates*), all but one group returned, at various times and in smaller numbers, after the sixteenth century. Only the Maronites lay claim to having always remained Catholic.

In 1443, Pope Eugene IV left Florence to move the Council a third time, now to the Lateran Basilica at Rome. There was the danger of the antipope, Felix V, elected at Basel, as well as the desire expressed by some to transfer the Council to the North again. It appeared safer to continue the Council in Rome to avoid any such moves; the transfer had the added advantage of putting the Pope closer to the source of funds for such a gathering. The Council remained in Rome from 1443 until 1445, the date usually set for its end. It accomplished nothing important that we know of. We are not even sure just how or when it ended. The fifteenth-century historian lost most of his interest when the Greeks departed for Constantinople. Apparently reunion with some other Oriental groups was effected, but this was done most probably by way of imitation, and out of fear of the Turks, with no lasting effect.

Meanwhile, in Constantinople, the work accomplished at Florence was rapidly coming to naught. The Emperor attempted to adhere to the agreement with the Pope, as did his successor; but the people were opposed. In fact, thirteen years later the emperors had not yet dared to publish the decrees signed in Florence; and all the while those opposed to union were violently attacking the notion. This included Scholarios, who had apparently undergone a change of heart; he had been in favor of union at first, but not at the close of the discussions. He had now become a monk and a most violent anti-unionist. The entire mentality of the period was summed up in the phrase: "Better the turban of the Prophet than the tiara of the Pope."

The next pope, Nicholas V (1447–1455), insisted that the Emperor publish the decrees, which he did. Nicholas also sent him what help he could. But it was already too late. Constantinople was doomed to fall. It fell to the Mohammedans on May 29, 1453, thus spelling the end of all hopes of lasting union.

Strangely, Mohammed II, who took over the rule, did not crush out the religion, as one might fear. Instead he chose to give the Greek nation a sort of autonomous organization under the direction of its religious leader. For this task, the clergy elected none other than Gennadius the Monk — the religious name of Scholarios. Thus the scene ended. Gennadius ruled only a few years, returning to his monastery in 1456, but the pattern was established and has continued until today.

While the Council of Florence, like II Lyons, failed to bring about a lasting union, it is remarkably indicative of the action of the Holy Spirit in a Council. Out of such a conglomeration of elements and cross motives, two particularly important results can be detected. One, the Church received its most clear and explicit statement concerning the doctrine on the Holy Spirit, a formula worked out in the discussions between the Eastern and Western theologians. Moreover, the authority of the Roman Pontiff that had been so challenged after the Council of Constance, now emerged more firmly established in doctrinal matters than ever before.

Unfortunately, the needed work of reform was never accomplished; it should have been attended to long before. All of these other concerns sidetracked this particular problem, however, but with tragic results. Very shortly the Protestant Revolt would break forth in full fury, to be met finally by the much-needed Council of Reform — Trent.

CHAPTER XIV ... *V Lateran — Trent*

ON THE eve of All Saints' Day, 1517, Martin Luther posted
on the door of the Castle Church at Wittenberg a printed card
stating a number of questions that he would debate in public.
Ever since, this has been considered the official beginning of
the Protestant Revolt. The movement, however, did not arise
that quickly; it was a long time coming, centuries long. The
nailing of Luther's 95 theses on the door of the Castle Church is
more a symbol of the movement than the actual start of it.

As men now look back on that troubled period of history,
they can perceive over the span of years various causes which
contributed to the entire effect. Catholics and non-Catholics
alike will agree today on the over-all situation. One cause was
certainly the corruption in the Church, the corruption above all
of the bishops and the popes. It is a striking fact to realize
that the Church could survive such a period in its history, a
period in which it was so often governed by men who had
little interest in the lofty spiritual aims of religion. When popes
and bishops become enmeshed in concerns for temporal goods,
in the pleasures of sex, in the political schemes of kings, the
entire Church suffers. The priests, as a result, were not well

trained nor particularly pious; monasteries had fallen from their ideals; and the laity were so neglected that they scarcely ever heard a sermon.

Nevertheless, throughout that period, great saints did arise and attempt to ward off the approaching crisis, and God did show that He was able to preserve His Church even under such conditions. Christ had foretold that the gates of hell would not prevail against His Church. Human weakness would not prevail either. The difficulty was that while some good was being accomplished, it was never enough. All the plans for reform drawn up at the Lateran Councils and afterward never achieved the full-sweeping reform demanded.

Just before Luther came on the scene the last such effort at reformation within the Church took place: the V Lateran Council (1512–1517). It is generally looked upon as a rather "weak" Council, not because of the positive steps it did take, but because of our overwhelming realization today of how insignificant those steps were.

Possibly those who took part in the proceedings failed to perceive the change in the air. A new world was in the making, but, in a way, the V Lateran seems to live out its days with an eye only to the past. The fifteenth century had been a great turning point in history. The Fall of Constantinople (1453) had brought with it a great influx of Greek scholars in the West; their influence inspired a new interest in the ancient culture of the Greeks and Romans — the Renaissance. This Humanism reached its golden age at the time of Pope Leo X. At this precise moment Luther entered the scene. The so-called "Renaissance Popes" were often the sponsors of the artistic and cultural works of Humanism, but this distracted them from their primary religious concerns.

At times, V Lateran gives one the impression of being an ecclesiastical literary society. Beautiful sermons were preached, excessive in their praise of the Renaissance popes. What was accomplished in regard to reform, however, was more or less an unsuccessful repetition of the other Lateran Councils of the twelfth century.

The immediate occasion for the Council was another schismatic movement, one associated with the so-called "Council of Pisa." This city had been an important name in the history of the Great Western Schism, and this might have been a similar threat. While the reformation movement was gradually forming itself, the Renaissance popes were once again engaged in the endless quarrels with Christian princes; this had marked the entire Middle Ages. This time Louis XII of France became irritated by the line of action followed by Pope Julius II and he summoned a "council" at Pisa in 1511. Fourteen or so bishops and four discontented cardinals attended. The meeting, a repetition of Constance and Basel, declared that the General Council was superior to the pope. It seems that Julius II had already thought of holding a General Council of his own; the act of the French King spurred him on. He convoked a Council to be held at Rome the following year. It was necessary to meet the action of the King and these bishops with a clear-cut response.

The Council at Pisa had actually never amounted to much; its threat to Rome was soon extinguished. The V Lateran Council opened on May 10, 1512, but was hindered from the start by wars, by the interference of kings, and by a general lack of interest in the Council to begin with. There were never more than one hundred or one hundred and fifty bishops who answered the summons, and these were mostly Italians. The sessions were separated at times by months. The first two were held in May, the third and fourth in December of 1512. When the next session was held in February of 1513, Julius II was dying, and the Council had to wait to be reconvened by the next pope, Leo X. Leo did this in April of that year, and a number of other sessions were held: April, June, and December, 1513; May, 1514; May, 1515; December, 1516; and lastly March of 1517.

What the Council did accomplish was the rooting out of the schism at Pisa. The most important discussions concerned the "Pragmatic Sanction of Bourges." In 1438 the King of France had issued this edict, affirming that a General Council was superior to the Pope, and denying the Roman Pontiff the right to nominate bishops in France. A later king had abolished this decree in 1461, but Louis XII had attempted to reintroduce it. The V Lateran Council clearly rejected the teaching contained in this edict; it thus contributed another strong statement concerning the primacy of Peter in the Church. In addition, a number of decrees were issued concerning certain philosophical errors, papal charities, and another crusade against the Turks. This last caused real concern outside of Rome; it was no longer the Middle Ages, and such an appeal met with no enthusiasm at all. The turn of events was to relegate such a venture to oblivion.

The V Lateran had closed in March of 1517. In October of that year, Luther launched his attack. As with many others, Luther shared in the spirit of the age that produced the Revolt. He too was concerned about the needed reform in the Church and upset by the laxity within it. At the start, he had not intended to leave the Church. But it became increasingly clear that the positions he adopted meant only one thing: a break with Rome.

From the start, the close relationship between Luther's position and that of Wyclif and Hus was clearly recognized; Luther and John Eck had debated that very point in their discussions at Leipzig in July, 1519. It was inevitable, since the very same causes had been operating to form the mind of Hus that produced Luther and the other reformers.

The general laxity of the Church was certainly one of the contributing causes. Luther finally chose as a solution the denial of the priestly office entirely. From this flowed his errors in regard to the nature of the Church and the sacraments. Another contributing cause was the strong emphasis on mysticism — the direct and personal approach to God. The individualism which so marks Protestantism reflects an exaggeration of the mystic spirit. The visible Church is considered as no longer necessary; it is even an obstacle, hindering the soul from its direct contact with God. This approach, accompanied with the recognition of general moral laxity, can easily lead to a full rejection of the Church.

There is a third cause recognizable in this movement: the decline of philosophy. The great speculative minds of the thirteenth century were now gone, and second-rate minds had taken their place; the result was a decadent Scholasticism. The general philosophy of the sixteenth century was what we now term "Nominalism." It was concerned more with words or names than with reality, hence the term — it comes from the Latin *nomen*, "name." Philosophers had now become tied to the words themselves, rather than what they stood for. They juggled them back and forth in various statements; they played a game with words, as it were. This too prepared the way for the Revolt. Luther is described as a fervent disciple of Ockam — a leader of the Nominalists. It was this above all that enabled Luther to formulate his teaching that a man can be sinner and saint at one and the same time. His faulty philosophy also had much to do with the position he adopted in regard to the presence of Christ in the Eucharist.

On the other hand, the decay of philosophy had introduced another note into the picture. Things had now become very much codified; philosophy had taken on a legalistic spirit. This state of affairs helped kill philosophy and tired men's souls.

When the interest of the Humanists presented a new concern for Scripture, and when the invention of the printing press made more Bibles available, men gladly turned to the simplicity of Scripture. It was so little codified that it pleased them. Translations of the Bible were made in most of the modern languages, which by this time had reached a fair amount of stability. Long before Luther appeared, there were German Bibles in print. This was all the spirit of the times.

Over in Switzerland a similar movement was under way. Two months after Luther was born in 1483, Ulrich Zwingli was born in Switzerland. He studied at Vienna and at Basel; in 1506 he became a priest. Zwingli was also influenced by Humanism, and he developed an interest in Scripture above all. About 1522 he came into prominence as a reformer, but he was not following the steps of Luther in this. He had shared the same spirit but came to his own conclusions. As a result, from the very start, the Revolt was divided into two parties; this division remains in Protestantism to this day, multiplied many times over. When, at a later date, Luther and Zwingli did come together to attempt some agreement, nothing was solved. They were divided especially on the question of the Real Presence, and they remained divided. Zwingli was also greatly opposed to images in church; Luther did not share this position.

The great name of the Swiss Reformation, however, was not to appear on the scene for another decade: John Calvin. He was born a Catholic in 1509, but set aside the faith of his youth about 1534. The Protestantism that he embraced, however, was more that of Zwingli than of Luther, to which he added his own special approach.

Lutheranism and Calvinism were thus the big problems of the sixteenth century. Luther emphasized that one is saved by faith alone, but to him this meant something more like "trust." Calvin stressed the free choice of God in salvation, so that only the *predestined* belong to the Church (those, that is, whom God had chosen for heaven). In Calvin's system this meant that all others were predestined for hell in the same fashion. In both movements, however, there was an acceptance of Scripture as the sole rule of faith; nothing else was needed. They held the conviction that Scripture was so clear that anyone who read it would immediately grasp the message. The obvious fact that they disagreed among themselves on certain passages failed to weaken this conviction; nor did they perceive any difficulty because of their mutual rejection of the scriptural interpretation of the Anabaptists (the forefathers of present-day Baptists), who rejected infant baptism.

To this was added also the defection of the Church in England under Henry VIII in 1534. Henry was not a part either of the Protestant movement or the emphasis on Scripture alone; he rejected papal supremacy because of his quarrel with the Pope over his marriages. Later on, others in England would introduce more of a Protestant element into Anglicanism, although even to this day it has not been identified entirely with the Protestant approach developed by Luther and Calvin. Scotland did adopt a Protestant faith in the Presbyterianism introduced especially by John Knox; this was derived directly from Calvinism at a time when Knox was living in Geneva. Presbyterianism, however, appeared about 1560.

This was the world that the popes of the sixteenth century faced, and it was an overwhelming problem. The whole Christian world seemed torn asunder, and entire sections of various countries had rejected the faith of Rome. The need for a reform within the Church, now far more apparent than ever before, could no longer be side-stepped. A reform from top to bottom was needed if anything were to be saved. The Council of Trent was to accomplish this task.

Trent, however, was not concerned solely with disciplinary

questions. Doctrinally it ranks with the great Councils of the first centuries. It added decrees on the nature of faith and justification that served to emphasize and clarify the primacy of grace that had been taught in the disputes with the Pelagians in the fifth century. The Council had set forth in precise terms the Catholic teaching on these matters as a response to the doctrine of Luther on faith, and of Calvin on predestination. Closely linked to these was the teaching of Trent on the theological explanation of original sin. The decrees on the sacraments, above all those on the Eucharist and on the Sacrifice of the Mass, have been directives for the theological progress of the past 400 years.

In discussing the history of Trent, we are faced with a mass of detail; it would take volumes to treat all that this Council accomplished. The Council lasted, on and off, for eighteen years: from 1545 to 1563. There were some lengthy interruptions, however. Leo X had been pope when Luther began his public preaching in 1517; he did condemn certain of Luther's teaching's in 1520, but this did not stop the movement. Adrian VI succeeded him in 1522, but he did not live long enough to do much. The first desire for the Council was expressed by Pope Clement VII, but he died in 1534 before anything was done. He reigned during eleven crucial years, but he was not the man to deal with the situation. He was possibly afraid of calling a Council; he was also by nature a man not given to making decisions. On the other hand, while he saw the need of a Council, the political situation may have been too great an obstacle. Clement is not entirely to blame for the delay.

Under Pope Paul III (1534–1549) the decisive steps were finally taken. Paul III surely ranks among the great popes of history. From the start of his reign he envisioned a General Council. He began with a reform of affairs at Rome, particularly in the Roman Curia (the papal court). From the members of the Curia considerable opposition was to arise. Even in times of crisis, when the entire world seems poised for collapse, there are always those selfish souls who think only of themselves and their own interests. This era was no exception.

In addition, the Christian emperors were to raise their usual difficulties; they continued to do so throughout the entire Council. Paul III finally did convoke a Council to be held at Mantua in 1537, but nothing came of it. There was still an interest in having the Lutherans attend, but they refused. At this time, of course, the lines between Catholic and Lutheran were still quite vague. Cities joined the Revolt only gradually, and sometimes almost imperceptibly. Thus one of the chief purposes of the Council was to seek reunion — a goal never achieved.

This stillborn Council was prorogued until the next year — that is, the Council was discontinued without being dissolved. The next attempt was to be held at Vicenza in 1538, but again nothing came of it. The Pope could not hold a Council if, after convoking it, no one showed up; but this is what was happening. The King of France kept his bishops from attending; the Duke of Mantua, where the first attempt was made, showed no real interest; and the German bishops were too harassed at home to leave. The French now also objected to Vicenza as a site for the Council. For much of this time, only the Pope seemed really interested in a Council at all.

In 1539, further attempts were made to reconcile the Emperor Charles V and the king of France, Francis I; they had continued warring, and were thus obstacles to the proposed Council. Attempts were also made to contact the Lutherans, but the many discussions proved fruitless. All of these negotiations went on and on, while from time to time equally fruitless attempts were made to convoke a Council. Not until the Peace of Crespy, in 1544, put an end to the war did the plans for a Council begin to take shape. In November of that year, Paul III issued a decree calling for a Council to be held at Trent (in northern Italy).

The Council finally opened officially on December 13, 1545. It had been hoped that the meetings would start in spring of that year, but it took all these months until a sufficient number of bishops were present. Even then the number was surprisingly small — about 30 bishops in all. The largest number at Trent was 199, the number who, along with other representatives, signed the final decrees 18 years later.

The history of this Council can be studied far better than many of the earlier Councils, thanks especially to the untiring efforts of Angelo Massarelli, secretary throughout the entire period. He is a delight to the historian because of his thoroughness, including at times such small details as a list of the food served at the banquets. The Acts of the Council also give a close account of the discussions and the voting; further insights are gained by the day-to-day diaries kept by Massarelli and others. In addition, the correspondence of some of the bishops has also been preserved.

The Council must really be divided into three periods: (1) under Paul III (1545–1549); (2) under Julius III (1551–1552); (3) under Pius IV (1562–1563). Because of the extreme length of the Council, the names that figure prominently change from time to time. Outwardly, the sessions were far more calm and orderly than some of the earlier Councils. Massarelli recounts a few small incidents, but nothing too upsetting. The best known is perhaps the reaction of one bishop to a rather critical remark he had overheard concerning his supposed ignorance in theological matters. The insulted bishop turned to his accuser and took hold of his beard with both hands giving it a good tug and extracting a few hairs in the process. The papal legates descended on them and put them both out for the time. But considering the upheavals of others days, this hardly merits mention.

In the first period, three papal legates presided: Cardinal Cervini, Cardinal del Monte, and Cardinal Pole; actually the first two dominated the proceedings. A manner of procedure was established by which the bishops (known as the major theologians) would gather together in groups under each one of the three legates. They would then discuss the decrees that had been suggested, and the results of these separate discussions would be reported in a united session later.

If a special problem arose, a vote would be taken. If further discussion was desired, the bishops could refer the matter to the so-called minor theologians (men trained in theology, but not bishops and not able to vote). The bishops could attend these discussions of the minor theologians, and thus gain further insights into the matters treated. When the decrees were finally formulated, a *solemn session* would be held, at which they would be formally accepted.

The first period included four solemn sessions in which decrees on doctrine and discipline were issued. The fourth session concerned Scripture and the apostolic traditions; the fifth, original sin; the sixth, the problem of justification; and the seventh, questions about the sacraments, Baptism and Confirmation especially.

Discussions had begun concerning the Eucharist, but other difficulties arose. For one thing, the Council was transferred from Trent to Bologna in March, 1547. Trent was far from a comfortable city in those days, and it was hoped that Bologna would be a more healthful and comfortable location. This move later became the occasion of disputes, rising from those few members who had not been in favor of the change; the emperor, Charles V, was strongly opposed to it. Wars and intrigue complicated the situation once more. Charles even hinted open opposition to the papal Council, with the ever present fear of schism. Because of these various difficulties, Paul III had decided to suspend the Council temporarily; his death, in November of 1549, closed this period of the Council.

After Pope Paul died, the Council continued in session long enough to elect the next pontiff; they chose Cardinal del Monte, the papal legate, who took the name Julius III. The new Pope soon indicated his intention of continuing the Council, but he too ran into difficulties. The next period did not get under way until 1551. The question had to be debated as to whether or not the Council would continue at Trent, and whether it would be a continuation of the Council of Paul III or a completely new one. Beneath this debate was the old theme of Conciliarism; the Emperor had challenged the right of the Pope to transfer a Council. Even in the face of the Protestant upheaval, the Church had to fight this error among its more faithful members.

Julius III won out, and the Council reconvened as a continuation of the first one. Cardinal Cervini was now rather ill; he could not continue as papal legate. This role was assumed by Cardinal Crescenzi, who was designated as the only president; two others were appointed as what amounted to assistant legates. On May 1, 1551, the first session of this new period — the eleventh session of Trent — was held. This time a number of German bishops also appeared, but the total number still remained small.

In this second period, short as it was, there were further discussions on the Eucharist and the sacraments of Penance and Extreme Unction; decrees were issued concerning them at the thirteenth and fourteenth sessions in October and November of that year. There was still some hope that the Protestants would attend the gathering; a number of representatives did actually arrive to attempt to make plans in January of 1552. By this time, however, not much was to be expected from such discussions; bitterness was strong on all sides. In addition, wars broke out again. The Emperor Charles had to flee to Innsbruck for safety, and because of this generally upset state of affairs the Council came to another end in April of 1552. Ten more years elapsed before it could be reconvened.

Julius III died in March of 1555, without being able to continue the Council. Cervini was elected Pope (Marcellus II), but reigned only from April 10 to May 1 when he died. Paul IV (1555–1559) then ascended the throne of Peter. This new Pontiff had no interest in a General Council; he had determined to reform things himself. His excessive measures, however, proved at least one thing: that a Council was needed to complete the work begun.

When Pius IV became pope in 1559, therefore, he began working slowly and patiently for the reopening of the Council. By April of 1561, the new papal legates were able to enter Trent. This time Cardinal Gonzaga served as the first president; Hosius, Seripando, and Simonetta were auxiliary legates. Although the Council was to have opened in April of 1561, there were not enough bishops present for many more months. Not until January 18, 1562, did the third period of the Council actually get under way. It was to prove the most difficult time of all, mostly because of the old problem of the Conciliar Theory. The discussions on the Mass and Holy Orders had been postponed time and again; now, as the work neared completion, these questions had to be faced. In doing this, the matter of the relationship of bishops to the Pope could not be avoided in the discussions on Holy Orders, which led to further difficulties. The complicated maneuvers of this period, however, cannot even be summarized here.

By the summer of 1562 the Pope was seriously considering dissolving the Council. By means of outstanding diplomacy, however, Pius IV placated all concerned, and in September it looked as though the Council would now hurry on to a peaceful end.

Such was not to be the case. The debates were renewed, and it became apparent that it was too dangerous to let things go on in such a troubled state. The Pope now sent on directions that the legates should drop all points on which no agreement could be reached, and have the bishops vote on those points which caused no trouble.

This did not hurry along the debates, however. Finally, in March of 1563, a change took place when a number of the leading figures died, including Cardinal Gonzaga, the papal legate. To replace him there came the hero of the entire session, Cardinal Morone — a man providentially prepared for this moment. Morone was the soul of diplomacy, and with the help of a few others, he was able to bring the Council to a peaceful conclusion, referring to the Pope all other matters over which they dared not delay.

The twenty-second session had taken place in September of 1562; the twenty-third now took place in July, 1563; the twenty-fourth came in November of the same year; and the twenty-fifth and final session on December 3 and 4. Throughout all of this confusion, the third period of the Council still managed to issue an amazing number of important decrees: one concerning the Eucharist; another treating of the Sacrifice of the Mass; the much-discussed question of the sacrament of Holy Orders was the topic of a separate decree. The last two sessions issued teaching on marriage, purgatory, indulgences, and the use of images.

As Cardinal Morone intoned the *Te Deum* of thanksgiving after the final signing, there was no question about the gratitude in the hearts of those present. In one of the most troubled periods in the history of the Church, the Council of Trent had effected the most far-reaching reforms, and this time they took effect. Pius IV solemnly confirmed the decrees of the Council, and set about completing the remaining tasks: the reform of the Missal and Breviary; the writing of a catechism based on the decrees of Trent; the appointing of a commission to issue a more exact edition of the Latin Bible (the Vulgate). This work was continued by his successor, Pope St. Pius V (1566–1572).

The Church had recovered from the crisis of the sixteenth century, but it was not able to undo the evil wrought by the Revolt. The sad remembrances are still with us today. The Western world sees the continued separation of those who rejected the Church 400 years ago. History looks back on the united Christendom that once was, and the Church of Rome looks to those separated from her with the sincere desire of reunion. As Pius XII explained, the Church waits for them with open arms to come "not to a stranger's house, but to their own, their father's home."

CHAPTER XV ... *Vatican Council*

WHEN the Council of Trent had completed its work in 1563, the world was fast becoming a new place in which to live. Within less than forty years, the new era would clearly overtake the human race. Today we speak of this as the Baroque Period (roughly from 1600 to 1750). A new spirit grew out of the Renaissance — a spirit of unrest, of progress, of grandiose ideals. It was the period of Louis XIV, of Newton and Galileo, of Descartes and Spinoza — all men who were to leave their mark upon "modern" civilization, for better or for worse.

In the life of the Church, this was a period of great reform — the Counter Reformation — during which men attempted to regain the ground lost by the revolt of the Protestant countries. It was the age of Bellarmine and Suarez, of Francis de Sales; it was the time when Milton and Molière came into prominence, the period of Rembrandt and Rubens, of Monteverdi and then of Bach. But this was also the age of the religious wars, of Gallicanism, and of widespread colonization.

Out of this conflict, however, there arose a second era which we now refer to as the Classic Period (more or less from 1750 to 1820). This came more as a reaction to the extremes of the post-Reformation period. It was a time of greater calm, when men turned once again to the ideals of the ancient Greeks — to the objective viewpoint, the emotional restraint, the clarity of form that they felt was expressed there. With this, however, there also came a greater emphasis upon man's intellectual strength; reason became king. Voltaire, Hume, and Kant reigned supreme; Mozart and Haydn attempted to express this spirit in music. The national spirit began to evidence itself, signified by the French Revolution, the Napoleonic Wars, the Declaration of Independence, and the American Revolution.

Even within the Church, this spirit of the "Enlightenment" became apparent. Reason tended to be overemphasized, and antiquity was idealized far beyond what it deserved. In 1794 a number of bishops, imbued with this spirit, gathered together at Pistoia, in Italy. This illegal synod attempted to promulgate decrees that failed to give due place to the visible Church, and which overemphasized the practices of antiquity; it was condemned by Pope Pius VI.

Finally, in the past century, we can distinguish the spirit of Romanticism (1820–1900), a further reaction to the cold intellectualism of the Classic Period. Men discovered once again that man is a living creature with emotions, with a heart. *Life* became the center of interest — the individual, the nation. The imagination took precedence over the intellect. While Beethoven, Brahms, Wagner, Tchaikovsky, Verdi gave vent to this spirit in music, Dickens, Goethe, Victor Hugo, Longfellow, and Poe expressed it in literature; Schopenhauer, Nietzsche, and Hegel introduced it to philosophy.

This was the Victorian Age but it was also destined to be the age of science. Perhaps the most convenient peg for this period is the publication of Charles Darwin's *Origin of Species* in 1859. Science had continued its development, and many felt that Darwin was the prophet of an entirely new era; some felt that this period marked a turning point in history: the end of religion and the reign of the scientific. While nothing so radical actually took place, these advances do exercise a tremendous influence on our present-day world.

Throughout all of these centuries, the Church had witnessed no other General Council. The decrees of Trent remained the law of the day, completed by the decrees of the Roman pontiffs. This last age, however, was to bring forth the twentieth General Council as an answer to the extreme rationalism and religious doubt that had been developing ever since the Revolt, and which came to a head in the nineteenth century.

The days of Luther and Calvin, of course, were numbered; Protestantism came rather soon to look upon them more as *symbols* of a movement than as religious teachers, in the accepted sense. The first Protestant creeds (such as the Augsburg Confession) became the norm or rule of Protestant faith; this is referred to currently as "Protestant Scholasticism." There was no longer an infallible teaching authority in a visible Church, but the Protestant notion of an "infallible Bible" had also proved wanting. The disagreements among Protestant groups were too apparent to be ignored. Thus these various creeds became the norm for the interpretation of Scripture; they took the place of the infallible Church rejected in the sixteenth century.

There were many revolts against this tendency, resulting in the formation of newer Protestant sects who chose as their starting point a return to the Bible itself. After Kant and the great emphasis upon reason in the Classic Period, however, the picture began to change more radically. The Enlightenment had so exalted human reason that it felt able to cast revelation aside; revealed truths were supposedly truths beyond the grasp of human reason, and this was unacceptable. Kant entered into the dispute in an effort to save faith and revelation, but his defense sowed the seed of further difficulties.

Kant accepted many of the conclusions of the men he opposed; he set out, therefore, to make a fresh start. When he had finished, there was no room in his system for the power of the human mind to know God by reason alone. In place of this, Kant had introduced the notion of an approach to God from *within* man himself. The inner experience of man was the important element.

It only remained for Schleiermacher to adapt this teaching to religion, and this came under the guise of a certain religious "feeling" or "affection." All religion was to be based primarily on some sort of inner awareness of God and the supernatural. Thus it was no longer the Church, nor the Bible, nor the Protestant Creeds that would determine man's belief, but only this inner experience, man himself. When Schleiermacher died in 1834, the stage was set for the errors of the nineteenth century that would demand another General Council.

To this notion of inner experience outlined by Schleiermacher, there was added a new approach to the Bible, known as biblical criticism. The Bible (no less than the teaching of the Church) was now to appear as an expression of the inner feeling of the Christian community. Thus the Bible had a gradual history, and upon occasion it even contradicted itself, depending upon the different "experiences" of the various communities. When this was combined with the main thought of the nineteenth century — that of evolution — Protestantism was faced with a full theory of the "evolution of doctrine" as a purely natural process. Christian faith was, in other words, nothing more than the end product of this experience of the community; it was a changing thing, and when the creeds no longer expressed properly the "present experience," the creeds should be changed. It is this line of thought that leads modern Protestantism to deny such basic truths as the virgin birth or even the divinity of Christ.

Ultimately this movement was to result in the nineteenth-century Liberalism of Harnack, for example, and in present-day Modernism. It is difficult to distinguish between these two. If we can at all, we might say that Liberalism began with the Christian tradition and made an attempt to adjust it to the new and changing world. Modernism, however, starts with the scientific method and investigates faith on that basis, more or less permitting traditional beliefs to take care of themselves as best they can. In neither instance, however, do we still retain a true Christian faith, a supernatural revelation of divine truths.

The Vatican Council stands out as the Church's greatest answer to the beginnings of this Liberal movement. About 1864, Pope Pius IX indicated his intention of summoning a General Council, the first in 300 years. Shortly after that, he issued an encyclical (*Quanta cura*) and a "Syllabus of Errors," both condemning the teachings of the modern rationalists and socialists. These, in turn, reflected earlier condemnations of the teachings of individual men. Gregory XVI, for example, had condemned Hermes in 1835 for his unwarranted exaltation of human reason, and Beautain, later on, for teaching that human reason could know about God only after revelation and faith.

In 1857, Pius IX himself had condemned the false rationalism of Günther, and the errors that resulted from it; and in 1862 he had condemned Frohschammer for similar teachings. These were all signs of an unhealthy acceptance within the Church of the errors developing in the Protestant thought of that day. They had to be stopped, and it was the Pope's desire that the forthcoming Council complete this task.

More time was needed to prepare this Council, however. In 1865, the Pope sought the views of a number of bishops concerning the advisability of a Council; the matter was as yet kept secret. In 1867, however, Pius IX announced his intentions publicly, and a congregation of cardinals began the work of preparing the decrees to be submitted to the Council.

To assist in this work, about 100 theologians from Rome and elsewhere in the world were associated with the cardinals. Some subcommittees were formed to discuss particular questions: doctrine; ecclesiastical and political matters; the missions and church reunion; church discipline; ceremonial; and religious orders. In this, the Vatican Council differed somewhat from Trent. At Trent the so-called minor theologians worked at the same time that the bishops held their discussions; it was hoped the work of the theologians would be finished, as far as possible, before the Council itself began.

In June of 1868, the Pope issued a solemn decree, convoking the Council and declaring that it should open on December 8, 1869. At this point, there was no special mention of the definition of papal infallibility. Nevertheless, the question was being debated at that time, and, long before the Council officially opened, the periodicals of the world were alive with discussion. The central question was whether such a definition would make the position of the Church more secure in the modern world, or prove a threat to its security.

Those who *favored* the definition were much concerned with the rise of Nationalism in those days, the ever recurring wars. There was a possibility that the Pope might be taken captive and exiled. They felt, therefore, that this definition would spell out more clearly the full authority the Pope would possess regardless.

Others, however, had fears that this was not the *expedient* thing to do. The world was so upset that this seemed to be an unwise move, inviting further disputes with the rationalists of the age. There were also some who apparently did not believe in papal infallibility — those who later left the Catholic Church when the doctrine was defined by the Council. The entire world, however, had witnessed the exercise of this papal infallibility in 1854, when Pius IX had solemnly defined the dogma of the Immaculate Conception; some 576 bishops had responded to the inquiry of the Pope before he took this step. What was being debated now was mostly a question of the expediency of the solemn definition of this papal infallibility.

The preconciliar discussion resulted from the "speculation" of the various newspapers concerning what would be treated at the Council. The result was a heated debate on the matter of defining this dogma. The foremost leader of those who considered the definition as not expedient at that time was Bishop Dupanloup of Orleans in France; Archbishop Deschamps and Cardinal Manning were strong supporters of the definition.

In Germany, however, a professor of history at the University of Munich, Ignaz Döllinger, was strongly opposed to the definition. He based his position on reason and history, and in doing so he lost sight of the infallible teaching authority of the Church. When the dogma was finally defined, Döllinger refused to accept the doctrine, and was eventually excommunicated. In 1871, he gathered about him a number of similar-minded men who spoke out against the "impudence and ignorance of Rome"; some of them set about forming a religious group of their own. They proposed to follow nothing but Scripture and tradition, and for them "tradition" meant history.

While these disputes continued, the work of the Commissions went on at Rome. The Council opened, as planned, in December of 1869; more than 700 bishops attended in all. They came from literally all over the world, so that considering the large number and the areas the bishops represented, the Vatican Council was surely the most outwardly "general" Council ever held. The meetings took place in the right transept of St. Peter's Basilica.

Pius IX had established the procedure to be followed. The preparatory Commissions were to issue the result of their labor

— a so-called *Schema*, which amounted to a suggested form for the definitions. These were printed and distributed to all the bishops. They had from eight to ten days to make in writing any observations they desired; these were turned in to what were known as the "Deputations." There were five of these, one which dealt with new topics to be suggested, and four others concerned with questions of faith, of discipline, of religious orders, and of the missions and Oriental rites. Actually, only the "Deputation of Faith" came into real prominence in the sessions; the Council had to be terminated before the other projects could be discussed. The preparatory work proved valuable, however, in later works of the Church, especially in the codification of Church Law in 1918.

The "Deputation" would decide if a particular suggestion were necessary or pertinent; the final decisions of the "Deputation" were ratified by the general assembly. It was in the so-called "General Congregations" (the ordinary meetings of the bishops), that the bishops discussed all matters. Every bishop was free to express his view; he had only to ask for a time when he might talk. As a result, over 420 speeches were given; about one fourth of them concerned infallibility.

These discussions labored under two handicaps. For one, the acoustics of St. Peter's left much to be desired. This problem was solved somewhat by the printing of the schemata and the suggested changes, but it was difficult to hear the speaker at times. In addition, Latin was the language spoken, and it was soon realized that the Latin pronunciation of the various nationalities was so varied that many could not understand the other bishops at all.

What was said at these General Congregations (there were about 89 in all) resulted in further changes in the decree being discussed. The suggested changes were distributed to all, and then one of the members of the particular "Deputation" concerned would explain the reasons why the "Deputation" either chose to accept or to reject the suggestion; after this a vote of the entire assembly would be taken on their decisions. It was in this regard that Archbishop Gasser became a prominent figure in the Council, since he spoke most often for the "Deputation of Faith."

When all had agreed on the final form, a public session was held. All the faithful were admitted to St. Peter's for these four public sessions: the opening session, and one for a profession of faith; and two at which the two decrees of the Council were formally promulgated — one in April and one in July of 1870.

Soon after the Council opened, the first draft of the decree on faith was distributed to the bishops. This was a long document, very complicated in nature; it evoked a great deal of discussion, lasting until January 10. It was then handed over once again to the "Deputation of Faith" to be revised. Toward the end of February, a greatly shortened version was ready; it included only the first part of the original version, four chapters in all. These touched on God the Creator, on revelation, on faith, and on the relationship between faith and reason. The discussion on this new version began on March 14, 1870, and lasted until April 12; for the most part, it was a rather calm and systematic discussion.

The final vote was taken on April 12, and on the 24th of that month the dogmatic constitution *Dei Filius* was solemnly promulgated in the third public session of the Council. The attention then turned officially to the question of papal infallibility. Unofficially, it had already become the dominant theme. During the very first months of the Council, suggestions had been sent to the "Deputations," asking that the matter of papal infallibility be treated; the discussions of the previous years indicated the need of this. Public discussion at the Council, however, was sidetracked until the decree on Faith had been settled.

Nevertheless, in January of 1870, the bishops had been presented with a schema on the Church. This was also a very lengthy document, treating of the nature of the Church, of the Pope, and of Church-State relations. This schema was indiscreetly passed on to certain periodicals, and this further complicated the matter; even the civil governments, who had not taken part in the Council at all, now became somewhat concerned over this proposed decree.

In the original schema, there was no mention of a definition of papal infallibility. Because of the desires of many bishops within the Council, however, a new section dealing with this question was added to the suggested schema. When the schema reached the open discussion stage, only one section was actually proposed — that on the Pope. The Council had broken up before the remainder of the decree on the nature of the Church could be treated.

Within the Council, the same divisions appeared that had been apparent in the periodicals. There were those bishops who thought that papal infallibility should be defined, and those who thought it was inopportune. It is important to remember that, at this time, papal infallibility was accepted throughout the Church. The heretical teachings of Constance and Basel were now ignored. The French clergy had issued a declaration in 1682 — the Gallican Decree — which had failed to give due place to the position of the Roman Pontiff; but by this time the decree had been set aside even in France. The opposition was based for the most part on the "spirit of the times," claiming that this made the definition ill-advised, and only invited further troubles. Actually, when the definition was issued, these effects which had been so feared failed to materialize generally; it was mostly an error in judgment in this regard.

The disputes continued within the Council both in private and in public; it was often a heated debate, and eventually a tiresome one also. In January, 1870, some 135 bishops indicated that they were opposed to placing the question of infallibility in the schema at that time; 27 of the 40 Americans were included in this group. The majority ruled, however. The discussions continued from January to April in private, and in the general sessions from April until July. Some attempts had been made to have the issue set aside while the Council was still debating the decree on Faith. But Pope Pius IX was insistent by now that the matter be treated. The reaction of some outspoken individuals outside the Council only confirmed the opinion of most of the bishops that the question had to be settled at once.

By March of 1870 it was decided, with the approval of the Pope, that the question be raised officially. On March 6 the bishops received an addition to the schema on the Church which proposed the dogma of papal infallibility. On May 9 the final constitution to be discussed was distributed to the bishops, and the debate began in the formal sessions.

This new version, vastly different from the very first one, contained only the section on the Roman Pontiff. It consisted of a preamble and four chapters, and included a solemn definition of papal infallibility. It had been reworked by the "Deputation of Faith" and the theologians who were serving as consultants.

By June 3, enough bishops wanted to close the debate to bring this about. The other sections of the decree were then discussed, and the final decree fashioned. By July 13 a final vote on the matter could be taken. This was the eighty-fifth session of the Council; 601 bishops were present; 451 voted in favor of the decree, 88 voted against it, and 62 voted in favor, provided that suggested corrections were made.

The fact that one fourth of the bishops had voted against the decree, or had at least limited their approval, caused considerable disturbance. Among this one fourth there were some very big names. It was clear, however, that the matter would be defined, and those who thought it inopportune chose the plan of quietly leaving Rome; in this way, they would not have to vote publicly against the decree.

When the final vote was taken on July 18, there were 535 bishops who voted in favor of the decree; two voted against it: Bishop Riccio of Sicily and Bishop Fitzgerald of Little Rock, Arkansas. These two immediately submitted to the new definition of the Church; the other bishops who had left Rome did so in the months that followed. In this way the Council answered the rationalists of the nineteenth century. These liberals had denied faith and stability in belief; the Church defined its precise notion of faith, and added to that its position on the doctrinal stability associated with the Roman Pontiff.

The next day — July 19 — the imperial government in Paris declared war on Prussia, and, for all practical purposes, this marked the end of the Council. The bishops had to leave, and only those from distant sees remained, in addition to the Italians. The number at the sessions went down from 136 to 127 to 104.

On September 20 the city of Rome had been invaded, and on October 9 the city had voted to join the Kingdom of Italy. Under these conditions, the Council could not continue, and any suggestions to move it to another city were set aside. Finally on October 20, 1870, the Council was temporarily suspended without being dissolved until a later but unspecified date. It was never reconvened after the death of Pius IX in 1878.

The Vatican Council had, nevertheless, achieved its primary goal and strengthened the Church by establishing a secure line of action for the even more difficult century that lay ahead.

Conclusion

THIS volume ends where it began: with an eye to the Council called by Pope John XXIII. Within the near future, the world will see this Council come to pass. It would be foolhardy to speculate on all that it will accomplish; time alone will tell. It will surely be the most outwardly "universal" of all the Councils, and surpass all others by the number of bishops who will attend. The progress of the modern world, the growth of the Church, the ease of transportation will make this possible. Nevertheless, as in the past, there may be some bishops who, because of political problems, will not be permitted to attend. The Church is not without such difficulties today.

In its sessions, the forthcoming Council will most probably turn its attention to those points raised, but never completed, at the Vatican Council. It can hardly avoid reviewing the doctrinal errors condemned by the popes of this century — that of Modernism, especially, which was so great a concern for Pope St. Pius X as well as Pope Pius XII.

Beyond this, we can be sure that the Holy Spirit will accomplish that which will most of all benefit the Church. Those who take part in the Council will have the history of these earlier Councils to guide them. Past mistakes can be avoided, and past successes imitated. But the modern world presents its own problems, and these will challenge the mind of the Council. There may be no easy solution to every problem raised. This was true in the past, and we have no reason to think that it will not be true in our own time.

Nevertheless, the world has every reason to look forward to this twenty-first Council with great interest. Viewing the accomplishments of the past, we may be sure that we are witnessing a great event in history. From this gathering there will come forth the directives that will guide the Chuch as it charts its path for the future. Once again, through the weak men who make up His Church upon earth, Christ will speak to the world. His Spirit, the Spirit of Truth, will once more guide the destinies of that Church in an extraordinary fashion.

Historians of the future will often look back upon these sessions; theologians will carefully analyze them. The Council will stand forth as a symbol of the Church in the twentieth century, that Church of which we ourselves are a part. It will take its place as the most recent addition to that long line of Christian landmarks erected through the centuries; it will give eloquent and lasting testimony to the abiding presence of that Divine Spirit promised by Christ. Through the power of this Spirit the Church has triumphed over persecution and heresy in the past, and through this same Spirit the Church will face without fear whatever trials may lie ahead.

Index

Index

Hypostatic union, meaning of, 47 f, 56

Ibas of Edessa, and Chalcedon, 63; and Constantinople II, 66 ff
Iconoclasts, defined, 83; effect of, 91; heresy of, 83 ff; and Nicea II, 85 f; and St. Methodius, 89, 92; in 16th century, 85
Idolatry, meaning of, 85
Ignatius of Antioch, St., 15
Ignatius of Constantinople, and Bardas, 92; exiled, 92 f; recalled to See, 94
Images, approval of, 88 f; worship and, 84 ff
Immaculate Conception, and Pius IX, 176
Infallibility, Church and, 9, 16; General Council and, 8; Pope and, 5; Pope Liberius and, 40
Infallibility papal, expediency of definition, 179; opposition to definition, 179; and Pius IX, 180; Pope Honorius and, 77–78; and Vatican, 175 ff; and Vatican Council, 175 ff
Innocent II, pope, and Lateran II, 108
Innocent III, pope, death of, 112; and Lateran IV, 111; and theology, 113
Innocent IV, pope, and Frederick II, 117
Innocent V, pope, Cardinal and Lyons II, 143
Innocent VII, pope, and Western Schism, 129
Irene, empress, and Nicea II, 86 ff

Jacobites, and Florence, 152
Jesuits, suppression of, 124
Joachim, abbot, heretic, 113
John IV, pope, and Monothelites, 75
John VIII Paleologus, emperor, 149; and Florence, 147, 150; and Photius, 96

John XXII, pope, and Spirituals, 126
John XXIII, pseudo-pope, 131, 133 ff
John of Antioch, 55
Joseph II, Greek patriarch, 148, 151
"Judaizing" Christians, 15
Julius II, pope, death of, 157; and pseudo-council of Pisa, 157
Julius III, pope, 167; and Trent, 166
Justin, emperor, and Monophysites, 67
Justinian, emperor, and Monophysites, 67

Kant, and modern Protestantism, 172 f
Knights Templar, 123 f
Knox, John, 161

Lapsi, problem of, 28
Lateran, councils of, reform and, 104 ff
Lateran I, 106 ff
Lateran II, council of, and antipope Anacletus II, 108
Lateran III, council of, and Albigensians, 111; and Frederick Barbarossa, 115; and Eastern Schism, 111; and papal elections, 111; and Waldensians, 111
Lateran IV, council of, and Albigensians, 113; and annual confession, 112; and Innocent III, 111; and Peter Lombard, 113; and Scholasticism, 112; and Waldensians, 114
Lateran V, council of, 156 ff; and crusades, 158; defects of, 156; and Leo X, 157; and Louis XII, 157; and papal primacy, 158; and Pragmatic Sanction of Bourges, 158; and pseudo-council of Pisa, 157
Leo II, pope, and condemnation of Honorius, 77
Leo III, emperor, began Iconoclast heresy, 83; crowns Charlemagne, 91; and Nicene Creed, 150; seized papal lands, 86

Index

Index

Index

Reformation, legalistic spirit, 159; and mysticism, 159

Renaissance, cause of, 156

Romanticism, 171

Sabellius, heretic, 18 f

Scholarios, a monk, Gennadius, 153

Scholasticism, and Lateran IV, 112

Semi-Arians, 38, 40

Semi-Pelagians, heresy of, 80 ff

Septuagint, Greek Old Testament, 22

Sergius of Constantinople, 73, 75; and Monophysites, 73

Servetus, Michael, heresy of, 138

Severus, Septimius, emperor, persecution of, 13

Siena, attempted council, 138

Sigismund of Luxemburg, king, and Council of Constance, 131 f

Simony, meaning of, 109

Sixtus III, pope, 55

Sophronius, and Monothelites, 74 f

Spirituals, Franciscans, error of, 125

State, Church and, *see* Church and State

Stethatos, Nicholas, and Cardinal Humbert, 100

Suarez, and Counter-Reformation, 170

Sylvester I, pope, and Nicea, 28

Tarasius of Constantinople, and Iconoclasts, 87; and Nicea II, 87

Tertullian, 18

Thaddeus of Sussa, 119

Theodora, empress, opposes Iconoclasts, 89, 92

Theodore of Mopsuestia, and Constantinople II, 66 ff; heretic, 46

Theodoret of Cyrrhus, and Chalcedon, 63; and Constantinople II, 66 ff; and Monophysites, 58; and Robber Synod, 60

Theodosius, emperor, and Constantinople I, 40

Theodosius II, emperor, death of, 60; and Ephesus, 54; favors Eutyches, 59; and Nestorianism, 50

Theotokos, meaning of, 47

Trent, council, 161–169; and Angelo Massarelli, 164; Cardinal Cervini and, 165; Cardinal del Monte and, 165; and Cardinal Morone, 168; and Cardinal Pole, 165; catechism of, 169; and Charles V, 163, 165, 167; and concerns of, 161; and conciliarism, 166 f; condemnation of Iconoclasts, 89; decrees of, 165 f, 168; and emperors, 163; end of first period, 166; end of second period, 167; and Eucharist, 162; and faith, 162; and Francis I, 163; and grace, 162; and holy orders, 167; and Julius III, 166; liturgy and, 169; and Marcellus II, 167; and Mass, 167; and original sin, 162; and Paul IV, 167; and Peace of Crespy, 163; and Pelagianism, 162; and Pius IV, 167 f; and Pius V, 169; Protestants at, 166; and reunion with Protestants, 163; and Roman Curia, 162; Scripture and, 169; and Trinitarian heresies, 43

Trinity, and Chalcedon, 61; and heresy of Abbot Joachim, 113; mystery of, 11; and technical terms, 16 ff

Uniate Catholics, 152

Urban II, pope, and first crusade, 112

Urban IV, pope, and Eastern Schism, 145

Urban VI, pope, and Anagni, 129; and Western Schism, 128 ff

Valentinian III, emperor, and Nestorianism, 50

Vatican council, 174–181; close of, 181; "Deputations," 177; faith